HOUSE
OF CARDS

HOUSE OF CARDS

A SELECTION OF
MODERN POLITICAL HUMOUR

EDITED BY SIMON HOGGART
ILLUSTRATED BY JOHN JENSEN

ELM TREE BOOKS: LONDON

ELM TREE BOOKS

Published by the Penguin Group
27 Wrights Lane, London W8 5TZ, England
Viking Penguin Inc, 40 West 23rd Street, New York, New York 10010, U.S.A.
Penguin Books Australia Ltd, Ringwood, Victoria, Australia
Penguin Books Canada Ltd, 2801 John Street, Markham, Ontario, Canada L3R 1B4
Penguin Books (N.Z.) Ltd, 102–190 Wairau Road, Auckland 10, New Zealand

Penguin Books Ltd, Registered Offices: Harmondsworth, Middlesex, England

First published in Great Britain 1988 by
Elm Tree Books

Introduction and Collection Copyright © 1988 by Simon Hoggart

1 3 5 7 9 10 8 6 4 2

British Library Cataloguing in Publication Data

Hoggart, Simon, 1946–
    House of cards: a selection of modern
    British political humour.
    1. Humour in English, 1945– – Special
    subjects. Great Britain. Politics.
    Anthologies
    I. Title
    828′.02
    ISBN 0-241-12451-4

Printed in Great Britain by
Richard Clay Ltd, Bungay, Suffolk

To Alyson

ACKNOWLEDGEMENTS

My thanks are due to Carol Keefer, for all her extra uncomplaining work, and to Caroline Taggart and Linda Longmore, who chased up articles I vaguely remembered, helped only by obscure hints, clues and inaccurate dates. And of course to the authors, who willingly allowed me to steal some of their finest material.

The Book of Fub by Michael Frayn was published by Collins.

The pieces by Frank Johnson are collected in the book *Out of Order* published by Robson Books at £7.95.

Honourable Member by Richard Needham is published by Patrick Stephens.

Westminster Blues by Julian Critchley is published by Elm Tree Books.

INTRODUCTION

Our kind of political humour is, I suspect, entirely British. The French either revere or despise their politicians, snubbing the middle ground where humour works best. American journalists take the concept of 'news' tremendously seriously and regard levity as an abandonment of their sacred First Amendment mission. Jokes are clearly marked 'humor' and are given their own playpen in a section of the paper named 'Style' or 'Living'. The idea of reporting an event in a way which pointed out its absurdity would horrify most American journalists, who are taught at college that if they ever mix editorialising with news, their mothers will be eaten by tigers.

In fact the present style of British political reportage, a mixture of mockery, scorn, scepticism and good honest cheap cracks, is fairly recent. Parliamentary sketches before the fifties tended to be reverent, even awestruck. Harry Boardman of the *Manchester Guardian* caught this tone with the title of his collected works: *The Glory of Parliament*. This contains a majestic reproof of Winston Churchill, but you realise that the old man's crime was to have let down the institution; there's no sense that the nature and structure of Parliament ever makes people behave fatuously.

Boardman was succeeded by Norman Shrapnel, a writer of immense elegance who loathed having to talk to strangers. This problem, which would cripple most reporting careers, made him ideal for the Parliamentary press gallery where he crafted some of the most elaborate, filigree metaphors ever seen on newsprint. If you are tired now of the House as repertory company, or Parliament as boarding school jokes ('"Ouch, yaroo!" cried the Opposition. Headmistress Thatcher was in a terrific bate . . .') you

7

can blame Shrapnel, who did it first, and best. MPs loved him, and on meeting him, would eagerly try to chat. After shaking hands, Shrapnel used to turn away, or in extreme cases leave the bar. 'Meeting them would spoil the purity of my hatred,' he would say. I've picked his farewell article for the *Guardian*, which expresses that purity in his wonderful, precise, chamfered style.

The first modern sketch writer was Bernard Levin, whose columns appeared in the *Spectator* during 1957 and '58. Though they were signed 'Taper' they were not pseudonymous, since an even then unmistakeable line drawing of Levin appeared with many of them. I sat alone in the *Spectator* library laughing out loud at his savaging of contemporary political time-servers – many of them already almost forgotten thirty years ago. Levin's style (or 'modus operandi' as it might be called) was the result of a conscious decision. 'My inspiration was,' he wrote in a letter, 'of all people, Shaw. Somewhere he wrote that he looked forward to the day when a reporter would go to Parliament in the way a theatre critic goes to the theatre – that is, he said, just as a theatre critic would not have a policy of crying up Irving and crying down Wyndham, and would think it very odd if he was expected to, so the Parliamentary critic would not be expected to support Conservatives or Liberals.'

Levin added: 'Eheu fugaces . . . it turned out that I couldn't do it literally; willy-nilly, I found I had a hero (Gaitskell) and a villain (Wilson) and a butt (Selwyn Lloyd), and a stoat-hypnotising serpent (Macmillan). But that's where it all began.'

Levin stopped writing Taper in 1958, and went on to become famous beyond the scant numbers of *Spectator* readers and Members of Parliament, who were probably his keenest followers. They almost always are. An MP is like an actor who has a first night every night, and needs to scan the review columns every morning. It is true that many of them take offence at what they read. One friend of a Labour MP once called me to tell me I had reduced the fellow to tears by comparing him to Michael Crawford, the actor. There's an irony: Crawford is now an international star, whereas the MP lost his seat some time ago.

It remains the case that if you make one enemy at Westminster, you automatically make 649 friends. As La Rochefoucauld nearly said, we all have the strength to read that our colleagues are blithering idiots. The sensible majority regards the occasional harsh word in their direction as a small price to pay for this daily pleasure.

It was the *Daily Telegraph* which kept the sketch alive in the 60s. Andrew Alexander was particularly effective against Ted Heath, whom he loathed almost as much as his friend and mentor Enoch Powell did. A typical Alexander column in the early 70s would begin with a withering attack on Heath's unimaginably asinine speech, setting off the glittering praise of Powell which followed. Andrew's effect was somewhat blunted by the fact that he had once tried to become an MP; they feel they can safely ignore someone who has tried and failed to join them. It's important both to be and to seem detached.

Andrew moved to the *Daily Mail* and was followed by Frank Johnson. The *Guardian* had lost Shrapnel, and after trying one or two others, settled down with Michael White. For nearly a decade (though Johnson kept switching papers and leaving the Press Gallery) these two were the best-known of all sketch writers. They were regarded by outsiders as deadly rivals, though I never saw any evidence of this in their personal dealings, and doubt if they felt it. Each had his own admirers, often for philosophical reasons. White was, and is, somewhat left of centre. Johnson, a well-read autodidact from the East End, is firmly to the right ('Mr Foot called Mrs Thatcher "the most reactionary Tory leader of this century". He was wrong. She isn't that good.')

Johnson went in for belly-laughs, or 'yocks' as they are sometimes jokily called in the trade. Spotting that the Labour MP Tom Litterick had taught economics at Dundee University, he invented the Dundee School, with its celebrated 'tree-grown theory of money'. There's a wonderful moment in his description, included here, of the Merseyside policeman failing to help his friend Michael Heseltine. Johnson also pioneered the extra-parliamentary sketch, which applies the same techniques as a column set in the Gallery to the real world. It works best only where you have the same ingredients as in the Commons: pomposity, windiness, self-consciousness without self-awareness. His favourite victim was Roy Jenkins, for whom he had a great fondness. This was reciprocated – always bad news for a political writer. I recall being mildly miffed to discover that Willie Whitelaw, seeing me arrive in Barrow to prepare the piece included here, phoned his friends to make sure they bought the *Guardian* next day.

White was usually more gentle than Johnson. His skill was rooting his sketches firmly in the political context of the day. You might not laugh out loud quite as often, but you were more likely to feel that a damaging point had been scored. Certain inanities would trouble him greatly – for example, Judith Hart's decision to become a Dame. She explained she had accepted 'on behalf of the Third World'. From that day on, White always referred to her as 'Sir Judith', a sobriquet which was hardly ferocious but pointed up the silliness of the whole affair. I've included the most famous of all White's pieces, the 'Gay Wedding' column from the 1987 election. It begins with a brilliant description of a Thatcher press conference – a short account of her style of government which could replace any number of ten thousand word profiles.

James Fenton is one of our leading poets and at the time of writing is covering the Far East for the *Independent*. He worked in Parliament in the mid 70s, and was a rare example of a reporter who could be as offensive about MPs to their faces as he was in print. 'Ha, ha, I thought you were a little over the top in your column last week,' the wretched legislator would say. 'Sorry, old chap, but on reflection I thought I'd been unnecessarily kind,' Fenton would reply, a very faint stammer masking some of the bluntness. MPs didn't know how to cope. Fenton attacked them from unexpected angles. Armoured against a frontal assault, they would feel a cattle prod up their backs. Take Sir Arthur Irvine. In 1977, it was assumed that any Labour MP in danger of losing his seat was a moderate hero, fighting off the evil Marxist left. The notion that he might be accused of simply not doing his job probably never occurred to either Sir Arthur or his friends.

Parliamentary humour can be difficult since so much of what passes for drollery in the Commons isn't funny at all to normal human beings. One way round this problem which Fenton discovered was to make it up. Not lies, but fables, short stories which communicate the truth better than a recitation of facts

10

could. Take his account of Roy Hattersley's visit to Bulgaria, which was based on a tiny kernel of truth, puffed full of air and coated with sugar, like the breakfast cereal. It works even better, since the piece is about the role of truth in politics.

One of my favourite Julian Critchley pieces is the one here about the 1984 Tory Party conference, which he missed. The whole thing is a fiction from start to finish, and more revealing than anything else I read about the whole sorry week. We newspaper hacks had mixed feelings about Critchley's arrival: we like to think of ourselves as litterateurs, whereas MPs write only for money. I do not blame them; these days they are paid rather less than the average greyhound racing correspondent, and Critchley writes with more grace than 99 per cent of full-time journalists. He has been criticised for re-cycling some jokes: you'll find here old favourites such as the 'Great She-Elephant' and the famous suede shoes routine. I do not complain; they are Critchley's equivalent of catch phrases, as much loved by his fans as 'Can I do yer now sir?' or 'Wakey, wakey'.

I have included work by a couple of people who are not strictly political writers, but occasionally turned their attention to the subject. Many of us who were reading the *Guardian* in the early 60s felt that nobody wrote as sharply and wittily about British society as Michael Frayn. This was in the days before the so-called 'satire boom' got underway. Frayn was not happy with the new trend, and attacked what he thought of as the cruel anarchism of *Private Eye*. Twenty-five years later it is Frayn's material which has weathered best: Christopher Smoothe, the Minister of Chance and Speculation, still walks the corridors of Westminster, now passionately loyal to Mrs Thatcher. As for Rollo Swaveley, the well-known public relations consultant, he has never been busier, though now he calls himself a 'parliamentary advisor' and holds parties attended by cabinet ministers.

Finally there are selections from people who are still writing the political sketch today: Craig Brown on *The Times*, Mark Lawson of the *Independent*, Ed Pearce on *The Sunday Times* and Andrew Rawnsley with the *Guardian*. It is, I think, too early to say who will be the best admired of these in the future; however, for the next few years, MPs will turn to them with justified anxiety while readers bypass the front page and the leading articles to find them.

At this point it is usual to express regrets to readers who cannot find a fondly-remembered column. I also apologise to writers who may feel themselves unfairly excluded. My only excuse is that some of the best political writing isn't actually *funny*; it may be cutting and trenchant, even sparkling with epigrams, but it isn't full of jokes. My one test has been whether an article makes me laugh. These did, and I hope you enjoy them as much.

HOUSE OF CARDS

One of Bernard Levin's first victims in the *Spectator* was Dame Irene Ward MP, an elderly lady most famous for her double entendres. She once complained that uniforms for female members of the Navy were being delayed until male ratings had been kitted out: 'Does my honourable friend mean that Wrens' skirts must be held up until all sailors have been satisfied?' she asked. No-one could ever be sure if she knew what she was saying.

'May I draw your attention,' said Sherlock Taper, 'to the curious incident of the Dame in the Question-Time?' 'But, my dear Taper,' replied Caradoc ap Watson, 'the Dame did nothing in the Question-Time.' 'That, my dear ap Watson,' was Sherlock Taper's reply, 'was the curious incident.'

And indeed it was. At Thursday's meeting of the 1922 Committee Dame Irene Ward had announced that unless she was satisfied by some member of the Government on the following Monday, she was going to create such a stir that she might be suspended. Dame Irene might have phrased her remarks more happily, as the prolonged guffaws which followed (they really will laugh at anything, those fellows) indicated, but there was a distinct rustle when, on Monday, Dame Irene rose to ask Question Number 7. She was dressed for martyrdom in a tasteful rust-brown costume, smart velvet hat, pearl necklace and ear-rings, and navy-blue accessories (it was not for nothing that I used to be Fashion Editor of *Hansard*); but horrid Mr Maudling ran away with the faggots just when the Opposition was leaning forward to toast marshmallows at the blaze. 'My noble Friend,' he said, 'is considering the representations my hon. Friend has made to him.' It did not sound like the fall of Jericho's ramparts, but those skilled in listening between the lines knew that Dame Irene was victorious. Her point had been that ex-municipal employees of the gas and electricity authorities were being treated more favourably, in the matter of pensions, than ex-company employees. Mr Maudling's noble Friend has now decided to tidy up the discrepancy, and Dame Irene marched down the House with the air of one who has diced with death and thrown a double-six.

Half an hour later Mr Butler was up to his tricks again. He slipped in just before the Prime Minister's questions were reached, tanned from Ghana's sun and wearing a summery suit and a bright blue shirt. Asked by Colonel Marcus Lipton whether the Prime Minister was not trying, on the question of doctors' pay, to tiptoe out of an impossible situation, Mr Butler replied that he wasn't, and that in any case the Prime Minister was not nearly so flat-footed as Colonel Lipton. Laugh? They nearly died. For what seemed like several minutes the laughter went on, renewed in peal after peal as hon. members who had got the point explained it to hon. members who had not. Order papers slipped from fingers too weak to hold them any longer, strong men on the front Government bench below the gangway got up and stamped on the carpet, Mr Alfred Robens repeatedly slapped his knees so hard that I began to fear he would give himself severe cartilage trouble, tears coursed unchecked down faces that had not laughed so much since the heyday of Dan Leno, and Mr Butler sat in the midst of it smiling modestly like a man who has just made a really good joke. Nobody, it seemed, had noticed that the remark had been another of the Lord Privy Seal's famous left-handed compliments. So the Prime Minister is not nearly so flat-footed as Colonel Lipton? I am sure Mr Macmillan is most grateful to Mr Butler for reassuring the House in this fashion.

Aching, they got on with the Army Estimates. The Defence White Paper being still a fortnight away, the debate wore to some extent an air of unreality, strengthened by the fact that Mr Hare opened it. Mr Hare is a convincing demonstration of Berkeley's theory of the non-existence of matter, for the moment he opens his mouth I become quite certain that he is not really there at all;

14

nor, to judge from the speed with which the House empties as he begins, am I alone in this view . . .

Next day they were debating herrings. Now I know a great deal about herrings, and in consequence there is only one man in Parliament whom I would listen to on the subject with respect and interest, confident that I could learn something from him. Sir Robert Boothby, however, was not expected to speak for some hours, so I strolled across to the House of Lords, much as a philistine with half an hour to kill in Bloomsbury might slip into the British Museum for a glance at the Elgin Marbles.

And a finer collection of Elgin Marbles than their Lordships I never expect to see. The studded red leather, the brass scrollwork, the devastating ugliness of the ceiling, the crested cushion on the Throne, the mobile hearing aids fixed to every seat, the Lord Chancellor's stomach, flowing gently over his knee-breeches – it makes a setting uniquely appropriate for the leisurely, somnolent, elaborate, inconceivably purposeless goings-on. Here a deaf Earl, there a gouty Bishop, content, not content, is it your pleasure, my noble Friend, amendment by leave withdrawn – on and gently on it went, until the inevitable happened and I fell into a sound and dreamless sleep. I awoke refreshed, to be rewarded by the sight of Lord Woolton entering, peering about him so like a short-sighted pawnbroker that I had half a mind to rush down the stairs and pop my cuff-links.

And yet, and yet. . . . The proceedings of their Lordships' House may not tend to any productive outcome; but they have a fascination entirely lacking from those of their rather more elected colleagues. Like the Tsarist Princes and Generals who became taxi-drivers and waiters in Paris after the Revolution, they exact admiration from us even as we shake our heads, with sad smiles, at the hopelessness of their case. The flag flies bravely from the masthead, though there is no breeze to make it stir. The widely-held belief that the House of Lords is a debating chamber of immensely high standards is no doubt a myth; but for entertainment tinged with nostalgia there is nothing like it. Besides, when they say a Bill is a bad Bill they give the impression that they mean it, and are not saying it because the Party expects them to. They talk their own nonsense in the House of Lords, and I for one salute them for it, though I think I shall not soon go back there.

BERNARD LEVIN
The Spectator, 1957

Hugh Gaitskell was leader of the Labour Party from 1955 until his death in 1963.

It is indeed fortunate that the penalty for falling asleep during a speech made by Mr Gaitskell is less severe than that reserved for those who sleep on watch in wartime. I wanted to hear the contribution made by the Leader of the Opposition to the debate on the Budget, and no soldier facing a court-martial and firing squad could have fought sleep as tenaciously and ingeniously as I did. I propped my chin on the point of my pencil (very painful); I ground the moulding on the woodwork of my seat into the small of my back; I so arranged myself that if I nodded off I would give my forehead a nasty knock on the edge of the desk. In vain; the spirit was willing, but Mr Gaitskell would have tried the fortitude of that saint (I forget his name) who was martyred by having his entrails wound upon a drum, and if martial law prevailed in the press gallery I would be saying 'To hell with the handkerchief' at this very moment.

It is not just that Mr Gaitskell was dull. If I fell asleep just because the speaker happened to be dull, my snores would long since have drowned the sound of Big Ben before the nine o'clock news. But the Leader of the Opposition spoke on the fourth day of a debate which deserved no more than one, and enough is enough. The practice of devoting four days to a discussion of the Budget, every imaginable aspect of which will subsequently be examined in microscopic detail and at microscopic length during the debates on the Finance Bill, is one which would have been absurd two centuries ago; the present state of the Parliamentary timetable being what it is, the custom seems little short of wicked.

Mr. Gaitskell making a point without fear of contradiction.

But it was not merely repletion that was troubling me. Mr Gaitskell's speech has been commended as being quiet in tone and detailed in content. Quiet it was, but it was not so quiet that my perfectly attuned ear failed to notice that it was in the wrong key. And I do not refer simply to his ghastly attempts at humour, which were about as amusing as the experience of having a tooth drilled by a drunken dentist. Mr Wilson had struck a chord earlier, and while most of the subsequent Labour speakers (we may omit Mr Allaun) had managed to harmonise fairly successfully, Mr Gaitskell struck up a solo rendering of 'Nellie Dean' which sounded incongruous indeed alongside the strains of 'Sweet Adeline'. Mr Wilson (a great little comic, that lad, by the way; could draw his forty nicker a week at the Chelsea Palace any time he wanted) had launched an attack on the Budget that roused the Opposition to transports of delight. But he combined the attack with a sober and carefully wrought examination of economic policy that roused me to transports of respect. That is exactly the combination I looked for from Mr Gaitskell; he is, after all, an economist of some repute, the leader of a political party, and a man with his country's interests at heart. Yet his speech lacked fire and profundity alike, and a less kind commentator than myself might have derived a gloomy prognosis of the country's well-being under a Gaitskell administration from his unfortunate reference to turning the ship of State hard a-port while his hands in the air swung an imaginary wheel hard a-starboard.

BERNARD LEVIN
The Spectator, 1957

Levin's description of Labour Party policy as 'a bargain struck between common sense and plain blithering idiocy' would probably be recognised by party members even thirty-odd years later. Sir Hartley Shawcross, who was Attorney-General and later President of the Board of Trade in the 1945–51 Attlee government, was famous for saying: 'We are the masters at the moment – and not only for the moment, but for a very long time to come', usually misquoted as 'We are the masters now'.

If Sir Shortly Floorcross is trying to get himself slung out of the Labour Party, he is going the right way about it. I would not go so far as to say that merely making a speech with some sense in it is now a proscribable offence, though occasionally, in the dark sleepless hours before dawn, I suspect that it will come to that. But the right hon. and learned Member for St Helens is nobody's fool; when he up and said that the new Labour Party policy of knocking off not whole industries but individual firms 'would lead the country to disaster', he knew precisely what he was about.

Now to begin with – though this will seem a trivial point to some of the faithful – he was right; it would. Nor need he imagine that he is the only one in the Opposition hierarchy who knows it. The trouble is, of course, that this policy is yet another of the appalling compromises from which the Labour Party suffers, the result of a bargain struck between common sense and plain blithering idiocy. Mr Gaitskell, for instance, who knows a hawk from a handsaw, should be perfectly well aware of the cogency of Sir Hartley's remarks, and may even wish he had been free to stand up and cheer when they were made. But the plan which came so signally under fire represents the best concession obtainable from a Left wing which, if it had had its own way, would have got ready to tuck a dozen major industries under its arm the moment Canaan hove in sight. The lesson which Bevin taught the comrades – that the Left could be met head-on and vanquished every time – was, alas, gradually forgotten as the long reign of Clement the First came to an end.

But I digress. Sir Hartley has made it plain enough, over the past few years, that he is not prepared to spend his time in the House of Commons. His division record would keep Crossbencher's 're- searchers' busy for weeks, and has me in transports of admiration whenever I contemplate it. For consider: at the Bar Sir Hartley could hardly have earned less than £30,000 a year. . . What is more – much more – he could then and can now employ his great mind and ability in crossing swords with immense and tangled problems; he could and can feed his restless, driving brain with the only meat such men think fit to eat – hard work; he could and can associate, as an equal, with the leading men of the land in all walks of life.

What conceivable advantages, for a man like that, has the idiot round of Parliamentary party politics? Why should he spend his time wandering about the sixth ugliest building in the British Isles, listening to the futile maunderings of his inferiors, eating vile food, breathing bad air, sitting cheek by jowl with cads? Ah, comes the answer pat, ambition should be made of sterner stuff; had he but set his mind to it, and played the game according to the rules, no political office in the land, nay, not Downing Street itself, could have remained closed to him. And to this I reply, in words that might as well be in Tamil for all the sense they will convey to some people, that Sir Hartley does not want to be Prime Minister. As far as I can see, he and I are the only two men in the country who would not take the office if it were offered to us. And why the devil should we? We are not suited to it, nor it to us. The hours are long, the pay meagre, the *cachet* fast disappearing. Whence Sir Hartley's freedom to call nonsense by its name, and whence, also, the ominous click of safety-catches. We have not heard the last of Sir Hartley Shawcross, Gent. But I think we have heard the last of Sir Hartley Shawcross, politician.

We have also, I trust, heard the last of Lord Salisbury, at any rate for some time. I did not myself have the pleasure of hearing his Suez speech in the House of Lords, but even in print it is the funniest thing since Rabelais, and hardly, in its talk of the country retaining the moral leadership of the world, more squeamish. For a puppet-master of Milord's supposed expertise, a Dapertutto of such cold-eyed and sinister efficiency, a maker and breaker of cabbages and kings, he has been guilty of more hamfistedness than even his greatest admirers (whoever they might be) can explain away. This is, no doubt, both irritating and bewildering to the Marquess. For years it could have been said of him, as Baron Corvo said of Father Benson, 'While he did not exactly aspire to actual creation, he was certainly of the opinion that several serious mistakes had resulted from his absence during the events described in the first chapter of Genesis.' Now he must be wondering what hit him. Well, I will tell him: Mr Macmillan hit him. Mr Macmillan is enjoying being Prime Minister, and wishes to go on doing so. He knows that the party would follow him now if he were to lead them smack into the River Weser, even without a pipe, and he is no more going to let a well-connected marquess get in the way of his meticulously rehearsed bonvivery than he is going to lose sleep over the faint grumbling that came from the back rank when he was careful to be seen splitting a bottle of port in the Carlton Club with Sir Victor Raikes. (What would they have had him do? Split a bottle of lemonade with Alderman Black or some other old wowser?) Besides, if I may adapt Bagehot to my purpose, the cure for an excessive admiration of Lord Salisbury is to go and listen to him.

BERNARD LEVIN
The Spectator, 1957

MPs' pay, and the majestic reasons they always advance for raising it, has been a generous gift to sketchwriters. Notice also Levin's splendid use of the unfair *attack anatomical*, in this case on the Earl of Home, then Lord President of the Council. The Democrats' crack that George Bush was 'born with a silver foot in his mouth' is thought to have been used against Lord Home thirty years before.

It is almost axiomatic that on those occasions when the House of Commons would tell you, if you asked it, that it was at its best, it is in fact at its worst. The case of the lolly (Mr Macmillan calls it 'emoluments') is a case perfectly in point.

It began on Thursday, with the Prime Minister's long-awaited statement. Indeed, so long awaited had it been that Sir Robert Boothby had been constrained, only the week before, to declare that if something wasn't said soon he would feel obliged to raise the matter on the adjournment – a threat so dire (for the temper Sir Robert would be in by half-past ten in the evening, particularly if something like the Finance Bill had been going on during the day, hardly bears thinking of) that pin-striped knees a-plenty could be heard knocking together, and the smile with which Sir Robert sought to undo the panic he had wrought only caused them to knock the harder.

Anyway, Mr Gaitskell finally rose to ask the Prime Minister, by Private Notice, whether he could now make a statement. The Prime Minister could and did. But observe with what skill he did it. No glad cry of 'Come to the cookhouse door, boys,' no jingling of the change in his pockets as he rose, no sly remarks about the right honourable and learned Member for St Helens not needing it: not even a bare recital of the facts and a resumption of his seat. The order of battle was: first, lean heavily on the Select Committee; second, lean heavily on 'exchanges between the Leaders of the three parties'; third, lean gently on ministerial salaries; fourth, lean on the Leader of the Opposition and the Chairman of Ways and Means and – well, not lean on, but at any rate brush against – Mr Speaker; fifth, lean on – nay, positively climb upon the shoulders of – the boards of the nationalised industries. Then sit down, remembering all the time that if you so far forget yourself as to wink at Mr Gaitskell Taper will notice, and not only notice but blab it all over the *Spectator*.

Mr Gaitskell's reply was equally correct. First, 'general satisfaction'. Next, particular satisfaction at – well, what? Why, Ministers' salaries, of course; Mr Gaitskell, though he will never make a strategist, improves in tactics every day. Finally, a gentle encomium for the Prime Minister and the Leader of the House and Mr Gaitskell sat down. He didn't wink either.

One hundred and twenty-two hours later (and don't forget that there was a weekend in the way) the Bill had received its second reading. No doubt about it; when the spirit moves these fellows they can move like lightning from the East unto the West. As for their Lordships, no sacrifice is too great when the public weal and three guineas a day are involved; they went so far as to sit on a Monday, and well over sixty of them at that. Whereat I grumbled mightily, but the chance of seeing the Earl of Home make a fool of himself (and there really is very little chance of seeing him do anything else) is one not lightly to be passed up. So there I was again, contemplating the Byzantine gilt from upstairs while the House of Peers was contemplating the Byzantine guilt from downstairs. Incidentally, Earl Attlee was causing a great commotion; happy in an expanse of red leather on the second bench, he suddenly decided to park himself on the front one, already crowded to suffocation (my word, Lord Silkin has put on weight these last few years!); to this end he wriggled and wriggled and wriggled, and gave poor Lord Stansgate's ribs treatment that a Harlequins lock-forward wouldn't stand for.

Then the Earl of Home, with the greatest possible delicacy, rose to explain to their Lordships about the scheme for paying their expenses, up to a maximum of three guineas a day. The only fault I could find with the noble Earl's exposition was that he seemed to be seriously in want of somebody to explain it to him first. I was, I may perhaps disclose, accosted in Battersea Park at four o'clock in the morning the other day, and reproached with being unkind to the Earl of Home. With a courtly bow I owned to the charge, but ventured to wonder what else it was possible to be to him. I was then informed that whatever the Earl's faults he was at any rate a solid fellow. This, I may say, I have never doubted; the trouble is that, as far as my own observations go, his solidity appears to begin at the fifth vertebra and to extend upwards to the *medulla oblongata*.

Next day, back on more familiar terrain, I sat open-mouthed while the House of Commons gave a display that would have made a hippopotamus retch . . . How important it was that the public outside the House should understand exactly why Members' pay was being increased! How hard they all worked, and for what meed of ingratitude! How much more MPs of other nations get paid! And – Pelion on Ossa – how expensive postage is! This last from a Cabinet Minister of the Government which is going to raise postal charges *next week*!

A little sense on the subject. MPs, considering the proportion of their pay that has to go on necessary expenses incurred in the course of their work, were for the most part clearly underpaid. It was therefore right and proper that they should help themselves to a little more, despite the length of the queue of people who deserve it far more than they would even if they worked as hard as they say they do. And short of a means test (Mr Butler would have called it 'undignified') this was the only way to do it. But did they really need to dress it up in so much cant? By the end of the display they seemed to be expecting a national vote of thanks for not making it a round two thousand. I fear that the pulse-

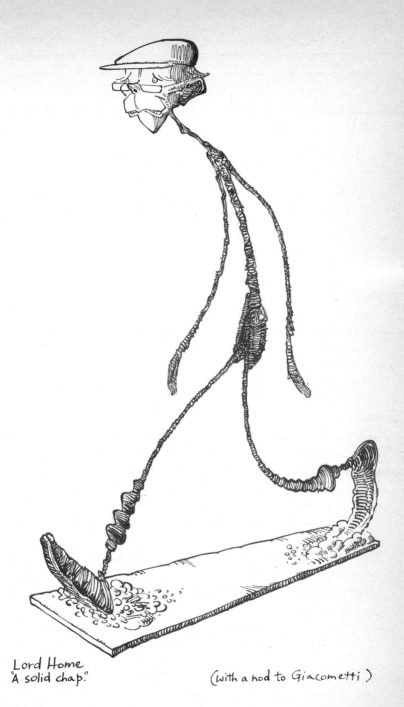

Lord Home
"A solid chap."

(with a nod to Giacometti)

25

takers have done their work ill; the nation seemed to me to be far less harrowed by the tales of MPs on the bread-line than the MPs themselves supposed. Poverty, after all, is relative; and there are some Members of whom one might say that it's no use supplying them with a bath, as they would only keep their gold in it.

Bernard Levin
The Spectator, 1957

Levin's favourite victim was Selwyn Lloyd, Foreign Secretary from 1957 to 1960, when he was made Chancellor of the Exchequer by Harold Macmillan.

Is not Christmas approaching, season of whatever-it-is and mellow whatever-it-is-fulness? Scrooge's nephew seemed to have the right idea: '. . . the only time I know of, in the long calendar of the year, when men and women seem by one consent to open their shut-up hearts freely, and to think of people below them as if they really were fellow-passengers to the grave, and not another race of people bound on other journeys.' So, as my taxi sped through the Christmas-laden streets of the West End at the speed of frozen lard flowing uphill, I determined that I, too, would open my shut-up heart, would look with a kindly eye upon those below me, would radiate goodwill.

Ah, but, you see, Scrooge's nephew had never heard the Foreign Secretary making a speech. After ten minutes of this perfectly dreadful stuff my goodwill had vanished with the last rose of summer. Hoylake UDC stood there, his pink nose a-quiver above his script, and read it out in a kind of plainsong chant, without the smallest trace of expression, understanding, or even interest. I have on occasion heard his courtesy impugned; he will not give way for interjections, it is said, as even the Prime Minister (albeit with a shockingly surly mien) will. On this charge, at any rate, Hoylake UDC is acquitted. He gives way so rarely because he simply does not see the Member who wishes to intervene; and he fails to see the intervening Member because he fears to raise his eyes from the text before him (even though, in this case, it was so bad that there seems to be the strongest likelihood that he wrote it himself) even for a moment, lest he lose what slight grip he may be lucky enough to have on the proceedings. Alexander Woolcott used to quote with relish an ineffable line from a thriller by William le Queux: 'The head of a murdered woman was certainly an odd thing for a man to be carrying in his luggage; the mystery had now assumed the proportions of a veritable enigma.' Well, the present Foreign Secretary is an odd thing for the Prime Minister – any Prime Minister, even this one – to be carrying in his Government; the mystery has long since assumed the proportions of a very veritable enigma indeed.

For – and this is something which only emerges clearly from a reading of the Foreign Secretary's speech, so infallible is his gift (a sort of inverted Midas touch) for making everything he says sound like nonsense – he was, by and large, right. His case was largely vitiated, it is true, and not merely by his delivery; like every non-swimmer he insisted on leaping in at the deep end, and was soon gulping unhealthy mouthfuls of chlorinated Marxism, Marxism being one of the many things Hoylake UDC knows nothing about. But when he said – I mean read – things like this: 'As we see it, there has emerged a consistent record of Soviet deeds since the war all pointing to a policy of expansion . . . they want to freeze the *status quo* in Eastern Europe . . . to split off Western Germany . . . to divide Europe from the United Kingdom and the United States, and to divide the United Kingdom from the United States. . . . A Summit Meeting which is an abject failure would increase tension rather than diminish it . . .' – when he said things like this, it is difficult to escape the conclusion that he was saying sooth.

Which only serves to make yet more inexplicable the enigma I mentioned earlier. For by the time he had finished . . . the Opposition had its fangs deep into the throat of the debate, and they did not thereafter let go. Yet it need not have been so; a Foreign Secretary who had displayed some interest in, and grasp upon, his theme might have tilted the whole balance of advantage the other way, and might even have roused a genuine feeling of enthusiasm for the NATO conference, even if not for the acres of pitiful twaddle that emerged therefrom.

Well, Mr Macmillan may ponder on his own troubles; but we have troubles of our own. For, bad though our present Foreign Secretary is, he is a great statesman compared to the alternative which faces the country if there should be an election and if the Labour Party should win it. Mr Bevan's speech was in one sense a triumph the like of which, all were agreed, the House of Commons has not heard since the greatest days of the Member for Woodford [Churchill]. At the end of this magnificent oration the Opposition cheered for minutes on end; on and on rolled the great wave of sound, gathering strength and volume and fierceness as it went. Wriggling with pleasure, as well he might have been, Mr Bevan sat amid the huzzas, while the Tories remained numb and silent, except for Mr Sandys who, possibly because he had just heard a very good joke or possibly not, roared with laughter. And yet I shivered as I listened to the Labour Party cheering, and Mr Gaitskell in his hammock and ten thousand miles away. For it is true that Mr Bevan had dismantled the Foreign Secretary and left him in pieces all over the floor; it is true that his oration (though, like many speeches which are great to hear, it does not read nearly so well) was a splendid succession of splendid periods, splendidly delivered; it is true that he faltered only once (when asked whether the practice of flying H-bombs on standing patrol had existed under the Labour Government, it was clear that he did not know, despite the fact that he was denouncing the Government for having been ignorant until the other day that it was happening now), and that he had one classic riposte. ('You cannot be deader than dead,' he declared, and when Mr Philip Bell – of course – interjected 'Dishonoured', Nye replied: 'All these terms are ceasing to be meaningful in this relationship, because honour implies a relation between a man and his social code, but if society is itself destroyed, nothing either honourable or dishonourable will be left.')

But when all was said and cheered, Mr Bevan's speech was what Mr Hagerty would call unadulterated rot . . . Mr Bevan has taken the opportunity of his Leader's absence to give the Labour Party a good, hard shove, not to the Left – for the instability of the party's latitudinal movements is notorious – but backwards; backwards, that is, towards the discredited idea of the Third

Force, of a great mediator who shall speak with tones of wisdom and breadth of understanding to both factions (the great mediator, it is hardly necessary to add, has silver hair and a Welsh accent) and in doing so may quietly, and with the best intentions and the sincerest of regrets, destroy the world.

BERNARD LEVIN
The Spectator, 1957

Julian Critchley, the most stylish of all MP-journalists, describes his first days in Parliament. It is said that some of Critchley's admirers can recall this turn verbatim, rather like Monty Python fans can recite the dead parrot sketch.

In October '59, when I first drove into New Palace Yard in my brand new Ford Popular, there was still something of 'Chips' Channon about the Tory Party. Today, the Tory Party in the House contains the Party Conference of ten years ago. Cheerful girls in hats who once moved conference motions in favour of corporal and capital punishment on behalf of the Young Conservatives of some Midlands town, small town solicitors and estate agents with flat, provincial accents, are now its Members. As Mrs Thatcher has gone up in the world, so the party has come down.

Twenty years ago you could tell a Tory just by looking at him. He was well suited. The party still retained something of its pre-war sleekness; elderly gentlemen in Trumper's haircuts, wearing cream silk shirts and Brigade or Old Etonian ties. Everyone seemed related to everyone else. I was for ever being accosted, when sitting quietly in the Smoking Room (the far corner of which was occasionally occupied by the grander Labour MP such as Hugh Gaitskell or Richard Crossman), by nice old buffers who claimed to have known my father. Many had had 'a good war', and one cure for contempt was to discover, while sitting in the Library during all night sittings, a slim volume such as *How I Rowed across the North Sea Singlehanded* by Sir Hugh Monroe Lucas-Tooth.

Within my first week or so in the House, I was sitting in the

Smoking Room reading a book. Charles Hill, who had spoken for me at the Chatham Town Hall during the election, came up to me. 'Young man, it does not do to appear clever: advancement in this man's party is due entirely to alcoholic stupidity.' I have taken care never to open a book since . . .

I sat uneasily in this assembly of bumblebees. Shrewsbury, the Sorbonne and Pembroke College, Oxford, enabled me, or so I thought, to pass for white, although of my grandfathers, one had been a railwayman on the London and North Western and the other a clerk in Bristol Gas Works. I gave up the stiff white collars that I had worn at the advertising agency and was careful to wear plain ties; but my suits were Burton's at £10 a time. One evening I was in the 'No' lobby waiting to file past the clerks to record my vote on a three-line whip. Out of a crowd of more than three hundred I noticed Sir Jocelyn Lucas, with whom I had never exchanged a word, making his way determinedly in my direction, and I watched him breast the wave like Captain Webb, twisting and turning. Could he be about to invite me to dinner? Or to congratulate me on my maiden speech? He took my elbow in the palm of his hand. 'You're wearin' suede shoes,' he said, and promptly vanished. Today we are all wearing suede shoes.

JULIAN CRITCHLEY
Westminster Blues, 1985

Psychologists suggest that some people subconsciously offer themselves as victims, whether to school bullies or journalists. Certainly there was something in Selwyn Lloyd's manner, or attitude, or phraseology, which made him a favoured choice of sketchwriters and satirists. In 1971 he became, surprisingly, one of the most successful post-war Speakers.

Lloyd

A HISTORICAL TRAGI–BUDGET, OR BUDGI–TRAGEDY, IN
FIVE ACTS

(Commissioned for the Hoylake Festival, 1994)

30

Act Three, Scene Four – a Chamber in the Treasury
(*Sennets and tuckets. Enter the Chancellor of the Exchequer, the Lord Privy Purposes, and the Lord Footstool, followed by Under-Secretaries, Parliamentary Private Secretaries, Joint Permanent Secretaries, Under-Secretaries' Private Secretaries, Joint Permanent Secretaries' Under-Secretaries, Fools, and Knaves.*)

Chancellor:
> I saw it in his eyes: he turn'd his gaze
> Upon me, wondrous soft, avuncular,
> Beseech'd me with those pouchèd eyes of his
> As might a man urge on his faithful hound
> To some high eager feat of houndly valour,
> Yea, with an uncle's smile he bade me forth
> To save beloved England's tottering cause
> With one bold coup-de-main of fiscal arms!

Under-Secretaries, etc.:
> Hurrah!
> > (*Trumpets, cannons, etc.*)

Lord Footstool:
> 'Tis well said, Chancellor, for Fortune frowns:
> And faceless men do undermine the boroughs,
> Unsettling vacant loons we once call'd ours.

Lord Privy Purposes:
> You mean to take a budget to our woes –
> To beat from metal tempered by the times
> And edg'd upon Necessity's hard stone
> A budget e'en to budget them to death?

Chancellor:
> I do. And with such high intent this day
> Are we three met to forge the cutting steel.

Lord Privy Purposes:
> Acquaint us with your strategems.

Chancellor:
> > > > Then hark:
> First will I ease the groaning discontent
> Which freights unjustly those our countrymen
> Whose lawful aspirations soar no higher

Than purchasing a humble toasting-fork.
Eleven per cent off toasting-forks, I say!

Lord Footstool:

This is a wise and bounteous act: the poor
Will count your name as blessed this day forth.

Chancellor:

Then will I buy the love of every man
Who holds the common mousetrap dear: the tax
On mousetraps swoops from nine to eight per cent!

Lord Footstool:

O admirable Chancellor!

Chancellor:

But now,
Our forces swoln by loyal mousetrap-men,
And grateful liegemen of the toasting-fork,
We fall like falcons on those jack-a-dandies
Whose foul-brained appetite doth feed on hats,
And scourge them with an added four per cent.

Lord Privy Purposes:

'Tis well. A hatted men is gallows-bait.

Chancellor:

And yet my devious strategem goes further –
Makes pepper-mills more dear, salt-cellars cheap,
Brings Jews' harps down, sends plated shoetrees up,
Puts two per cent on fire-dogs, cheapens pins,
Tacks tax on tacks, attacks the tax on ticking.

Lord Privy Purposes:

Hurt barrel-organs, Chancellor, I pray –
Their monkeys satirise us publicly.

Chancellor:

Why, so I will. Yet list, we do proceed,
These hair's weight-balanced dispositions made,
These plots complotted, nimble gin-traps sprung,
At last to strike the boldest blow of all!
And gentlemen not in the Treasury
Will count themselves accurst they were not here
To ride forth on St Crispin Crispian
And cry: Fifteen per cent on lollipops!

Under-Secretaries, etc.:
> Hurrah!

(*Trumpets, cannonades. The Chancellor of the Exchequer draws his red dispatch-box from its scabbard, and holding it aloft gallops off in the direction of Agincourt.*)
Lord Privy Purposes:
> Such hair-springs drive the clock of destiny:
> Small wonder it still stands at ten to three.

MICHAEL FRAYN
The Book of Fub, 1963

A televised House of Commons has been a recurring fantasy for humorous writers; see Oliver Pritchett's article on page 116.

Housebiz

I wonder if a little more interest in politics might be aroused if politicians cast modesty aside and displayed that total self-absorption which film stars always seem to be able to put over so effectively in interviews. Well, here's a trial run I did with Mr Nigel Sharpe-Groomsman MP, star of Parliament and Tory Party Conference.

Good morning, Mr Sharpe-Groomsman.

Call me Nigel, Mike.

Nigel, you're appearing at the moment in the Infectious Aliens (Exclusion) Bill, aren't you?

That's right, Mike. It's a fearless, controversial bill, of course, but it's immensely human and worthwhile. My role is to stand up and speak out in favour of the brotherhood of man. Of course everyone thinks I'm letting the side down, but in the end I turn out to be loyal after all when I produce horrifying figures of Danes and Dutchmen arriving with influenza, and I vote with the Government.

It sounds a great debate, Nigel.

Yes, it is. The bill's being introduced by my old friend Chris

Smoothe. He's a wonderful, wonderful politician, and it's been great fun working with him on this. But then the whole team is absolutely wonderful, and I think we've produced a wonderful, wonderful bill that everyone's going to enjoy a lot.

Is this the first bill you've done with Christopher Smoothe?

No, we were in the Landlord's Protection Bill together in 1960, with Harry Debenture and Simon Sheermurder, and again this year in the Welfare Services (Curtailment) Bill, which broke all records in gross savings at the Treasury. Landlords' Protection, of course, was my first starring part.

You've certainly shot to the top, Nigel. Nigel, is it true that you were first discovered modelling for men's wear advertisements?

Yes, I got my first break through the photograph that caused all the scandal – the one of me in underwear and suspenders. A Conservative Party agent saw it and snapped me up at once.

Tell me, Nigel . . .

Call me Nige, Mike.

Nige, you've sometimes been described as the new Harold Macmillan.

Yes, Mike, I have. But I've also been called 'the new Duncan Sandys', 'the new Ernest Marples' and 'the new Lord Salisbury'. I don't like these labels. I should like to be thought of just as myself, Nigel Sharpe-Groomsman. I mean, after all, I'm fundamentally a person in my own right. That's what I want to get over.

You don't think there's any truth in the labels, then?

Oh, I wouldn't say that. I think it's true that I have Duncan's nose and Ernest's legs. But people say I smile like Harold Macmillan. I don't think that's entirely true. When I smile – so I'm told by many critics and political commentators – my whole face lights up in a very individual way. And I don't want to get typecast. I don't always want to be the sort of member who appears to let the side down by talking about the brotherhood of man but who always rallies round and votes for the Government in the end. I mean, I want the public to realise – I want Ministers to realise – that I'm a serious politician. It's not that I haven't enjoyed doing this wonderful, wonderful Infectious Aliens (Exclusion) Bill with Chris, but one has one's career to think of.

34

"I'm a serious politician."

One last question, Nige. . . .

Call me Ni, Mike.

What sort of bill would you most like to appear in, Ni?

Well, Mike, I'd like to do a bill which offered a role with a greater chance to express the real me. A war bill, for example, with a debate where I call for courage and sacrifice from the nation in face of overwhelming odds. I mean, basically I'm the Churchill type. My friends all tell me I've got Churchill's ears.

Thanks for coming along, Ni. I'm sure we'll all be watching you tomorrow in the Infectious Aliens (Exclusion) Bill.

MICHAEL FRAYN
The Book of Fub, 1963

Few people caught the way politics had become a branch of public relations so quickly or so accurately as Frayn. He was perhaps helped by working outside the House, where a reverence for tradition is easily confused with a respect for reality.

Christopher Smoothe's Wall Fixture

Mike, old boy (*said Rollo Swavely, the well-known public relations consultant*), you gave us quite a nice little spread over that bingo debate, and frankly I should like to do something for you in return. Have you ordered, by the way? They do an awfully good tournedos here, you know.

The point is, Mike, I've got a story that's rather up your street. I'll be putting it out to everyone tomorrow, but I thought you might like to have it today – for old times' sake, and strictly off the record, of course. You remember I have the personal account for Christopher Smoothe, the Minister of Chance and Spec? Well, he's going over to Berlin next Friday to visit the Wall.

Oh no, old boy, he's not the last – I don't think the Minister of Ag and Fish has gone yet. Anyway, here's his programme:

36

12.00 noon: Arrive Tempelhof Airport. Met by Federal Minister of Bluff and Counterbluff. Exchange speeches about West's faith and ideals.

1.00 p.m.: Lunch with leading West German armaments manufacturers. Gives speech about necessity of remaining strong in face of the Communist threat.

2.30 p.m.–2.45 p.m.: Applause.

3.00 p.m.: Drives in state procession to the Official Wall Viewing-point.

Now here's where we're going to need a bit of very delicate timing. The Official Viewing-point has a fantastically busy schedule, of course, and it's booked up for months ahead. They only managed to get Christopher in at all by cancelling Cynthia Stocking, the former prospective Deb of the Year. Even so, he's timed to arrive at 3.35 – only a minute and a half after the departure of the last visitor – Rock Richmond, the famous rock 'n' roll singer. (Incidentally, I hope this burgundy's not too jejune for your taste.)

3.37 p.m.: Official Guide explains history and architecture of Wall, pointing out in particular any features of chance or speculative interest.

3.40 p.m.–3.43 p.m.: Mr Smoothe looks at Wall.

3.44 p.m.: Mr Smoothe mounts to viewing platform and looks over Wall into East Berlin. Uses panoramic direction indicator marking principal political prisons, etc. Official Guide directs his attention to any secret police arrests, forced labour, mass starvation, or other signs of repression which are to be seen, depending on visibility.

3.47 p.m.–3.50 p.m.: Mr Smoothe lost in silent contemplation.

3.51 p.m.: Mr Smoothe is photographed looking into distance with compassionate expression.

3.52 p.m.: Mr Smoothe is photographed turning back towards West with look of determination to preserve the solidarity of the Western alliance.

3.53 p.m.: Overcoming his evident emotion, Mr Smoothe speaks.

'When I came here today,' he will say, 'I little guessed how deeply – how very deeply – I should be moved by what I saw. But now, thanks to those brave and selfless West Berlin carpenters who erected this viewing platform, I have seen the Communist world at first hand. I have seen, with my own eyes, what look for all the world like the streets, the houses and the people we know so well and love so dearly in the West. But what a terrible difference there is! I think I need only say that whereas we are on this side of the Wall which you have shown me with such heartfelt hospitality, they are on the other side.'

It's a rather short speech, but at four o'clock precisely the next VIP, Walter Wagstaff, the Free World Showbiz columnist of the 'New York Herald-Angel,' is due at the Official Viewing-point. But later on in the day we hope Christopher will return to the Wall and switch on a chain of giant loud-speakers to inaugurate the Free World Bingo Game. The calls should be audible all over East Berlin, and we hope resistance workers will smuggle the cards in and out.

Well, that's the programme, Mike. (Shall I order another bottle, by the way?) It should nail those absurd stories that Christopher's not deeply and passionately interested in human affairs. There's only the tiny worry I have – and this of course really is off the record – and that's exactly what we'd do if the East Berliners built a viewing platform on *their* side of the Wall, and started running VIP trips to stare at Christopher and the rest. I know it would seem absolutely unbelievable cynicism to us, but I wouldn't put it past the Communists to use a situation like this for the purposes of propaganda.

MICHAEL FRAYN
The Book of Fub, 1963

Like Frayn from the centre-left, Peter Simple attacked politicians obliquely from the right. Michael Wharton, who wrote the 'Way of the World' column in the *Daily Telegraph* until he retired in 1987, rarely wrote directly about politics. He drew on his own vast reading – and also tapped the collective unconscious of educated, traditionalist folk to comment on current events. Like Frayn, he was uneasy with the modern world, though, like many conservatives, rather more pessimistic.

A great debate

Moving the second reading of the Discrimination (All Purposes) Bill, Mr A. Grudge (Lab, Stretchford North) said that if Britain were to maintain her standing in the eyes of the non-aligned world and move rapidly forward into the Space Age, it was essential to stamp out all vestiges of discrimination whether on grounds of race, sex, religion, age, moral character, intelligence or anything else.

It was intolerable, to give a few examples, that one-armed Pakistani women were excluded from the Oxford Boat Race crew; that magistrates, in open court, publicly discriminated between honest people and so-called criminals; that Calvinistic Methodist children of low intelligence were excluded from the higher grades of the Civil Service.

We must build a Britain in which everyone pulled together. If we could not make everyone alike (and personally he hoped that Science would soon make this possible), at least we should treat them alike.

Sir Rufus Grunt (C, Natterhurst) said that he hoped the Bill would deal with the possibility of flogging everyone, not merely violent criminals, periodically. A good sound tanning never did anyone any harm; if he might say so, he was himself a living proof of this. If he could not get anyone else to flog him, he flogged himself every day.

Miss Edith Sandpiper (Lab, Shuffham) complained of sex discrimination in such places as men's Turkish baths, which deliberately excluded women. She herself, as a test case, had recently entered a men's Turkish bath in London. At sight 'of her all the customers fled and one of the attendants fainted (*laughter*).

Sir Rufus Grunt: They thought she was a Turk (*laughter*).

Mr A. Grudge: That is a perfect example of the sort of racial discrimination we are trying to deal with. How would the Hon. Member, if he were a Turk, like to have such offensive remarks made about him? (Labour cries of 'Cyprus!' 'Suez!' 'Smethwick!' etc., etc.)

Wing-Cdr H. J. Wolfram-Jones (C, Nerdley) said that the problem of discrimination was closely bound up with juvenile delinquency, road accidents, old age pensions, the 11-plus examination, steel nationalisation, alcoholism, indecent films and the present flood of printed filth. He believed that unless this country devoted itself to the ideal of service it would perish, as the Roman Empire perished. But he did not think more motorways and shorter licensing hours were necessarily the answer.

The debate continues.

PETER SIMPLE
The Daily Telegraph, 1964

Norman Shrapnel's farewell article. He continues to write for the *Guardian*, though one rarely senses that he misses Parliament itself.

Keeping order in the House

How can you bear it, my more compassionate friends used to ask, sitting up there day after day, year after year, listening to those politicians? For a long time – decades, it should have seemed, though a decade is really a short time in British politics – the question never occurred to me.

Then, ready as the next man for a stimulating bout of self-pity, I began to have nasty visions. Old Commons order papers laid themselves end to end and reached to the back of the moon. Fat White Papers whom nobody loved began to advance in formation behind a massed skirl of ten thousand Scottish questions. And all those permutations and confrontations played themselves out anew, over and over: Macmillan and Wilson, Home and Wilson, Wilson and Home, Home and Heath, Wilson and Heath, Heath and Wilson, Heath and Thatcher, Wilson and Thatcher ... Then I realised that few people could stand it, day after day after day. Certainly no politician could. No wonder they have jobs outside, or queue to get put on committees.

What clinched it was meeting a man I hadn't seen for many

years. 'You must,' he said accusingly, 'be the doyen of the Parliamentary sketch-writers by now.' It struck home. Find yourself at the receiving end of a word like that and you never know what they may be throwing at you next. Clearly it was time to go. But the last thing I want to do is sound churlish. I am grateful for the privilege of having been in on all those political seed-times and harvests, those seasonal returns of Harold Wilson and rotations of Fred Peart, that long line of Speakers stretching out (as it now seems) to the beginning of time . . .

What effect – this was quite the most daunting question I have been asked – did all those years of listening to Parliament have on my political philosophy? Though tempted to answer in the manner of the late P. G. Wodehouse, that if the world was looking to me for a political philosophy then it was going to be one political philosophy light, I suppose I can at least claim that I came away with a few maxims and observations – all learned the hard way, all tested and warranted sound at the time of delivery and worth their weight in ink.

To the best of my observation, and contrary to popular prejudice, British politicians are far from being layabouts. Indeed, most of them busy themselves to a dizzying and sometimes irresponsible degree – irresponsible, because the best and most apparently conscientious way of dodging major challenges, like the collapse of the total economy, is by immersing yourself in minor ones, like the decline of the traditional tennis-ball-cover industry at Little Weaving . . .

By the same token, the busiest Ministers are often the least effective. They tend to go to earth in their little red boxes. The most valuable politicians and the rarest, among Ministers and Shadow Ministers and backbench MPs alike, are those who sit back and think. (Merely sitting back, however, is not enough.)

One thing that has baffled and frustrated me through all these years of parliamentary reporting has been that the politicians you like most are often those whose views you least appreciate, and vice versa. Likeability, all the same, remains one of the great snares of British politics. Lacking for the most part the coarser and more tangible sweeteners available to lesser breeds, MPs are tempted to compete in the popularity stakes which can be a more harmful sort of corruption. A good backbencher has got to make a permanent nuisance of himself, for non-egotistical and non-office-seeking reasons. (This doesn't mean, necessarily, that he won't *get* office: the system will stop at nothing to disarm original thinking.)

As soon as political opponents start saying, 'But he's a good chap at heart,' a man needs to watch out. That old urge to be loved is a seductive drug and has destroyed more political talent than drink or women. The reverse of the same bad coin, the urge to be disliked, is less dangerous because more obviously perverse.

Of all political honours there is least justice in the Gift of the Silver Tongue. Seductive rubbish will always bring them crowding in – to the Press Gallery not least – while dull, sensible, well-informed speeches are constantly being made to a virtually empty House. Obviously the flight from rhetoric has gone too far. Language still counts but it is not in a good state, and people with something to say should look to their tools of communication. Orwell used to maintain that the first signs of corruption showed in the language, and he may still be right.

The slump in national and political self-confidence has also led to a dangerous nervousness towards new ideas. When Dick Taverne, years ago now, ventured to suggest, with all due tact and restraint, that the day might come when we would need to stop regarding the inevitability of economic growth as part of holy writ, some MPs regarded him as guilty of heresy, sacrilege and indecent exposure rolled into one. Who would have thought that Mr Wilson would soon be producing his DRINK ME bottle for the nation to swallow – doctor's orders and no argument – making our chins sink to our boots almost overnight?

As for the changing ritual of the Commons, the more significant variations must be left to the political historians and social psychologists. (Why have they stopped rolling their order papers page by page and fitting them together into long, thin wands? This used to be the main occupation of tedious debates, all-night sittings and the like, but I haven't seen anybody doing it for years. Many of the old wand-makers are now in the Lords. Then why don't they carry on the industry there? I think I know the answer to that: it's because the Lords order papers are so small.)

Gone with the wind, too, is the old convention that required new members to blush their way through their maiden speeches with a modesty that would have been judged overdone in a mid-Victorian débutante at her first ball. Now they are allowed, even expected to address the House with their natural brashness on a subject they actually know something about. A change entirely for the better, I'd say.

And what, from the videotape of memory, are the things that stay in the mind – things they did, things they said? The sequence is vivid but strange, as though edited by one of the few surviving surrealists in current affairs. Harold Macmillan, leaving the Chamber, turns with lofty scorn and bows as they mock him. (What can *that* have been for? Obviously something somebody else had done.) Walking chess-players perambulate the division lobbies during an all-night sitting. The ancient Churchill, in his last days, steers his way to his place below the gangway like a stricken battleship, petulantly shaking off the tugs that try to guide him.

'Actually,' a peer is saying in the Upper House – they were the first words I ever heard uttered there – 'one of my best friends was a cannibal.' His patience exhausted late one night, a distinguished Liberal, later still to become a distinguished peer, is complaining that something or other he has been listening to in the Commons is 'nothing but piss and wind'. The only Communist peer, a farmer named Lord Milford, is making a speech in the House of Lords recommending the abolition of the House of Lords and is voted a bit eccentric.

Our politics, whatever they say, remain predominantly personal. Mainly it is the one-man shows you remember. Sydney Silverman, that tiniest of great backbenchers, ending capital punishment virtually single-handed. Enoch Powell, late one scornful night, lashing his Government over the 'disaster' of the Hola affair. John Profumo, whose own affair was before long to bring the Tory house down, making his personal statement to the Commons. Black Rod, that historical and elegantly costumed messenger from the Lords, interrupting a Commons debate at an unfortunate moment and being set upon by furious backbenchers, a scene as astonishing as if an MFH were to be attacked by the hounds. The saturnine Tom Swain, crossing the floor to slap an evening paper in front of Ted Heath, informing the then Prime Minister that the unemployed had officially topped the million mark.

That scene – nearly three years ago now – led to an uproar that made Speaker Selwyn Lloyd suspend the sitting. This eliminated Prime Minister's Question Time and spared Mr Heath a cross-examination on, among other burning topics of the day, unemployment. That kind of built-in retribution is one of the charms of the place, though it tends to get called other things.

So goodbye Westminster, farewell Parliament Square. The place has never been boring and will no doubt go on producing its normal crop of astonishing surprises. Perhaps even the monotonous, mildly hectoring Margaret Thatcher will blossom into the Meir of our politics. Perhaps British Labour will settle into its golden age of sanity under Crosland, or some such. Perhaps Thorpe will be king one day. From now on, they must sort it out for themselves.

NORMAN SHRAPNEL
The Guardian, 1975

In March 1976, Harold Wilson unexpectedly resigned the leadership of the Labour Party. Roy Hattersley, another gifted writer-MP, has the misfortune to have become a butt: see Peter Simple's piece on page 77. Denis Healey was also one of Fenton's most frequent targets, though so widely did he spread the abuse in his *New Statesman* column that it would be unfair to describe any single victim as a 'favourite'.

The Balkan Nightmare

Let us begin in Bulgaria. As you may be aware, Mr Roy Hattersley, the Minister of State for Foreign Affairs, left London on his official visit half an hour before the Prime Minister announced his resignation. Arriving in Sofia, he was met by the Foreign Minister, who appeared somewhat agitated. 'Mr Hatterjee,' the poor man said, 'we are most honoured that you should visit us at such a time. We do hope, however, that your plans will not be affected by the *resignation of the Prime Minister*!' 'On the contrary,' said Hattersley suavely, 'I feel that the love and respect between our two countries is a much more important matter than any question of mere politics. I intend to go ahead as planned – as long as you are agreeable.'

This statesmanlike reply caused immense delight among the Bulgarians, and the visit went ahead as planned. You know the sort of thing – a guided tour of a barbed wire plant, a dreadful encomium from the president of the Writers' Union, interminable folk dances, and in the evening – a champagne reception. At which, the Foreign Minister came up again. 'Mr Rattersley,' he said, 'you must realise how grateful we are that you have not altered your plans as a result of the Prime Minister's resignation.' 'Please don't mention it,' said Hattersley, 'it really makes no difference at all. But tell me – there's one thing I don't understand. Why does the Prime Minister play such an important part in your constitution?' After a stony silence, the Foreign Minister laughed softly and nervously. 'Mr Battersby,' he said, 'there appears to have been some mistake. It is not *our* Prime Minister, it is *yours* who has resigned.' The champagne glass fell from Mr Hattersley's hand.

This story (I have sketched in some of the details, and I'm afraid I lied about the champagne glass) is more or less the truest thing that I have heard over the past week in the Palace of Westminster. Everyone is lying through their teeth. It's a game. As Mr James Wellbeloved said in the tea-room on Monday, rising from his armchair and dusting off the crumbs: 'Well, I think I'll just go along and feed those dumb-fool journalists some more phoney information.' And I am reliably informed (not by Mr Wellbeloved) that when the campaign managers got together and added up the number of firm commitments they had received, the total figure came to considerably more than the number of Labour MPs – 427, to be precise. There is a rumour that a cross check is going to be made, to expose the proven liars.

In some cases, there is good reason. Poor Mr Geoffrey Robinson, the new Coventry MP, appears to have been considerably badgered. I was told by a Benn-man: 'He's voting for Benn on the first ballot and Foot on the second. I didn't bully him – I just said – look, Geoffrey, you've been in the Labour Party for some time, you know what's what, more than some of these sods. And we had a little discussion, and at the end he said, well, he thought he'd probably vote for Benn first and Foot second.' So the story got around that Robinson was voting for Benn, and then a counter-story was put around, saying he was for Foot. By Tuesday night, when I got to him, Mr Robinson had not voted. He was undecided, he said. As a matter of fact, he looked absolutely terrified . . .

The campaign so far has been fairly cleanly fought. There is of course a certain amount of black propaganda flying around. The enemies of Jenkins put out a story that Jenkins had threatened to sack 50 mediocrities as soon as he came to power. At once, the mediocrities were in arms, and the Jenkins-men had to scotch the rumour. So far from being against the mediocrities, they said, Mr Jenkins is positively in favour of them. He's running on a mediocrity ticket. Several people are getting worried about their future, and you can't move in the Palace of Westminster without bumping into placemen, jostling for position. Jostle, jostle, all day long . . .

The main attempt in Westminster at the moment is to find some formula for stopping Mr Callaghan. Whether it will succeed is, as far as I'm concerned, a matter for earnest, hopeless conjecture. For instance, the Jenkins-men were saying that if Mr Jenkins came second to Mr Foot in the first ballot, then all the soggy Centre would go rushing to make things up with Roy. Whereas the Healey-men were saying that under these circumstances there would be a Gadarene rush for Healey. Mr Healey has, after his unpropitious start, made up a certain amount (if not enough) of lost ground. He has tried, also, to wash his mouth out; and wild horses would not drag from me the name of the candidate who, when asked 'Mr X, if you win, what would be your biggest headache on becoming Prime Minister?' replied – quick as a flash – 'Mind your own bloody business!'

JAMES FENTON
New Statesman, 1976

He has tried, also, to wash his mouth out.

It is surprising to realise that this column, which attacks among other things sucking up to the Americans and excessive government secrecy, was written in a Labour government and not during the past nine years.

What the Queen Really Said

MY LORDS AND MEMBERS OF THE HOUSE OF COMMONS.

My Husband and I are appalled at the events being prepared to mark the 25th Anniversary of My Accession to the Throne. However We realise that We will have to go through all the palaver in order to keep the nation sweet, and to preserve our share of the money supply. Anybody who imagines that the Jubilee would be an appropriate occasion for a nice gesture (such as reopening the grounds of Buckingham Palace, which used to be available to the public, or handing over Our magnificent art collection, which was all bought with your money) has another think coming.

My Government is determined that it shall not be blown off course. But if it is blown off course, it is determined that it shall not be seen to have been blown off course. For if it is seen to be so blown, it will lose the confidence of the nation. For this reason, all compasses, charts and log-books will be declared classified material, and withdrawn from general use.

My Government will maintain its abject servility in all matters relating to American foreign policy. Whatever Mr Carter decides to do will be perfectly okay by Us, thank you very much.

My Government will continue a level of defence expenditure which is out of all proportion to our economy ... My Government will continue to take part in ridiculous and costly war-games in the North Sea. What ships we have will continue to potter round the globe, causing vast amusement wherever they go. My army will continue to train for an active role in domestic emergencies.

My Government will remain compliant with the wishes of the CIA. My Home Secretary will shame us all by his deportation orders, which will be designed to make this country as unfriendly as possible towards alien champions of liberty and justice.

Their domestic counterparts will get pretty short shrift as well, if My Government has anything to do with it.

My Ministers will continue to govern under conditions of maximum secrecy, so that the left hand will not know what the right hand is doing, and so that it will remain more or less impossible to find out who is taking the major decisions, and on what evidence the relevant judgments have been made . . .

My Government will continue to permit any old foreign chancer to move in and buy up our national newspapers without referring the matter to the Monopolies Commission or lifting any other sort of finger at its disposal.

My Government will continue to make the break-up of My Kingdom as slow, lingering and painful as possible. Any thought of giving way gracefully or efficiently will be stamped on.

In this, and over elections to the European Assembly, My Government will proceed only with legislation that has been forced upon it by circumstances beyond its control. In consequence, the next session will be dominated by Bills for which there is no genuine enthusiasm within the elected body.

My Government will continue to appoint rich nonentities to the boards of public sector industries and will continue to feign surprise when they turn round and bite the hand that fed them. In this connection, We note with interest the progress that has been made towards the abolition of the British railway system.

Under no circumstances, be it understood, will My Government introduce a wealth tax. Those few of us who have a bit put by against hard times are in no mood to share any of it out with the masses, and it happens that we are in a position to make our views on the matter well understood.

In these trying times, you would hardly expect Us, would you, to raise the question of the public schools?

And don't imagine, despite the muttering of My Lord President, that anything will be done about the House of Lords. It still suits my Government to bribe its aged members with the occasional peerage. This practice will continue into the foreseeable future.

My Ministers will also continue in their firm and principled opposition to any form of coalition, until such time as a better offer is made, or they are forced by actuarial considerations to have a little chat with that nice Mr Steel . . .

My Government will continue to campaign for the equal treatment of human beings, irrespective of colour, race or creed, excepting when such human beings are trying to get into My country.

My Ministers will stand by the collective decisions of the Cabinet, and the collective decisions of the Chancellor of the Exchequer and the collective decisions of the Prime Minister, and will not indulge in any public or private criticism of those decisions. There will be no opportunity for public discussion of alternatives until the opportunity for implementing the alternatives has passed away. My Ministers may then approach the publishing houses and obtain contracts for their memoirs.

My Ministers will take every possible precaution against being thrown out of office or going to the country. If such measures begin increasingly to look like the measures proposed by My Leader of the Opposition, then so be it.

Other measures will be laid before you.

MY LORDS AND MEMBERS OF THE HOUSE OF COMMONS.

I pray that the blessing of Almighty God may rest upon your counsels.

Or, failing the blessing of Almighty God, I pray that I should be allowed to be among the first to board the life-boats. After that, it's every man for himself, and the last one out's a rotten egg!

JAMES FENTON
New Statesman, 1976

Another prescient column. 'Radical Alternatives to Sex' which Fenton invented, became a common shorthand way of referring to Young Liberal foolishness.

The Death of the Silly Party

There was a time when the Liberal Party was the Nutters' Party. It welcomed all and sundry, provided all and sundry could demonstrate that they were more or less irredeemably beyond the pale. All the fads of the Labour Party and all the shortcomings of the Tories, the eccentricities of the English Nationalists, the dottiness of the Scots, the loopiness of the Welsh, the fantastic behaviour of the Cornish separatists – all, one might say, of the pied beauty of British politics was found in the Liberals. A haven of utter silliness in a wilderness of sanity, they were there to amuse, to entertain, to divert. Some of them were born silly, some achieved silliness, some had silliness thrust upon them. But by God, at the end of the day, when the chips were down, they were silly.

A word about this word 'silly'. . . It really needs a little definition. First of all, there's nothing wrong with silliness. In origin the word is Anglian – *selig*. It means nothing more than happy, or innocent, a meaning it retained in its Middle English form *sely*. As far as I know, the last example of this correct usage (but perhaps readers can come up with more recent ones) occurs in *The Rime of the Ancient Mariner* (1798):

> The silly buckets on the deck
> That had so long remained,
> I dreamt that they were filled with dew
> And when I woke, it rained!

The buckets were silly, not in the sense of stupid, but in the sense of innocent. The buckets were *not guilty*, like the Ancient Mariner himself, of shooting the albatross. They did not partake of any responsibility. They were innocent, says a note in my edition, and therefore blessed.

In exactly the same way, the Liberal Party used to be silly. The decades passed, administrations rose and fell, reputations were made and lost, successive Chancellors eased and squeezed the economy, the furniture vans arrived in Downing Street, new curtains were ordered, carpets were worn down, manifestos were abandoned and pledges were pledged – but the Liberals were not responsible. Sometimes, like the silly buckets, they filled with dew, or filled with dew in the dreams of guilty men. There were the great revivals – Orpington, and a couple of others. But these, like rainfall, were nothing to do with the buckets themselves. They just happened, and the Liberals would get very excited. Now, however, all those happy days have passed, and for the Liberal Party the Age of Silliness is well and truly over . . .

Now it was clear, from the moment that Steel took over the Liberal Party, that a mortal blow had been struck against silliness. One looks back on his election campaign as a great final fling: John Pardoe's platform, with its delicious irresponsibility – 'What this party needs is a real bastard – vote for me'; and then the ingenious way Steel proved himself an even greater bastard by telling the press that Pardoe's hair wasn't real. It was a looking-glass version of the normal political campaign, with each candidate trying to prove himself worse than his rival. It was silly, all right, but the silliness was unilateral. The triumphant candidate was chronically well-behaved. Try as he might, he could not actually be silly.

Few of those who attended the Liberal Assembly last year noticed the change that had come over the party. The delegates continued to behave as if nothing had happened. All over Llandudno their orange badges proclaimed that something harmless and amusing was going on – a commission on microdevolution, a meeting of Gays against Fluoridation, an Esperantist coffee morning. There was street theatre (*The Trial and Acquittal of Peter Hain*), morris-dancing and a lecture on 'Radical Alternatives to Sex' . . .

But there is a dangerous point in the life of a political group when a sense of destiny, a spirit of seriousness, begins to take over . . . It is like that moment when Caligula asks Claudius whether he can see the change, and Claudius has to guess what on earth Caligula means; he stumbles around for a moment, and then suddenly realises that Caligula has become a god.

In the same way, the Liberal Party had ceased to be silly, but nobody realised until they were told. Pardoe continued to behave as if he were still silly. On Budget day, he was all for Healey's

The death of the Silly Party.

package. The next day all bets were off. The Liberals were going to bring down the Government, themselves, the pillars of the temple, the lot. After that, it took all Steel's skill at back-pedalling to save the situation. Watching him on Thursday night as the Stechford vote was being counted, as Robin Day (clearly exhausted by anticipation) absentmindedly asked him what he thought of the three major party leaders, I could not help feeling sorry for his predicament. For, as a serious politician, he had chosen rather the wrong moment to 'come out'.

JAMES FENTON
New Statesman, 1977

Sir Arthur Irvine was appointed Solicitor-General in 1967. He died in 1978.

Sir Arthur Who?

This column has a deep, primitive, almost atavistic respect for old age. It believes that grey hairs in general bring wisdom, and that wisdom in general is worth having around. It believes that, in cases where the behaviour of the old becomes tiresome and eccentric, every allowance should be made for infirmity. Old people have different systems. They work according to different routines. For instance, although they tend to sleep less soundly than this column at nights, they are often grateful for a kip during the day. And why not, for heaven's sake? Haven't they earned it, one way or another, over the years?

But this column would be less than realistic if it did not recognise that the old are sometimes inclined to take advantage of the deep, primitive, almost atavistic respect in which they are held. For instance, I cannot help thinking that the Rt Hon. Sir Arthur Irvine, PC, QC, MP, would be pushing his luck if he relied too heavily on the deep, primitive, almost atavistic respect of this column. I have no personal animus against the man. I've never met him. All his colleagues emphasise his niceness; some of them remember his abilities; none of them can understand why he is kicking up such a fuss.

For of all the recent cases in which a constituency has tried to get rid of a Member, the case of Sir Arthur Irvine *v.* Liverpool Edge Hill CLP seems the clearest cut. It has been running now since at least 1971. Every year there have been rumours that Sir Arthur is to be ousted. Sometimes it has looked as if the question was settled. Then, miraculously, the old boy would stage a comeback. A couple of years ago he was on the *Daily Telegraph*'s list of high-minded moderate MPs who were in danger of being pushed out by wicked left-wingers. Now, however, he will find it very difficult to gain the martyr's crown. If he is kicked out, he will have only himself to blame.

For he has been spectacularly idle. It is said of Rossini that he was once composing an overture in bed when the manuscript slipped to the floor. Rossini was so lazy that instead of getting out of bed to pick up the half-finished work, he abandoned it and started another overture from scratch. Sir Arthur, during the whole time that his future as an MP has been in doubt, has set similar standards for parliamentary inertia. His legal practice may have been thriving (his most interesting recent case was that of Graham Young, the St Albans poisoner, whom he defended) and you may have read of his reputation for speaking incredibly slowly, and at incredible length – so much so that lawyers involved in the same cases as him have been known to celebrate their good fortune in advance with bumpers of champagne.

However, when it comes to the Palace of Westminster, this one-man Jarndyce case is the soul of brevity and wit. His last session of frenzied activity was 1970–71, when he spoke for ten minutes on the Courts Bill, nine minutes on the European Community, a similar amount of time on the sale of arms to South Africa, made two more interjections and put one oral question. This effort appears to have utterly exhausted him. In 1971–72 he made two speeches, amounting to less than one column in *Hansard*. The next year he made another two, the year after none at all. For all this period I can find no written questions in his name. In 1974, between February and October, he rallied – he

55

spoke three times. After that, I have failed to find any oral contribution in his name. On 3 March last year, in a rare written question, he asked the Secretary of State for the Environment 'if, in his forthcoming transport policy review, he will lay down the criteria to be applied to the consideration of proposals to run down particular rail operations and to close depots' – but the answer supplied by Dr John Gilbert, a veiled 'No', seems to have finally discouraged him. Perhaps his distress was observed, for three weeks later we find in *Hansard* that 'Mr Lambie asked the Secretary of State for Scotland if he will pay an official visit to Irvine'. Nothing came of this unusual idea.

He has, of course, done a certain amount of voting – but not much. When his presence is required in Westminster he may be found, his colleagues tell me, meditating upon affairs of state in the library; in order that he might concentrate better, his eyes will be closed, his jaw will sag, and perhaps a slight noise, somewhat like a snore, will escape his mouth. O Dennis Skinner! O Ian Wrigglesworth! O Robert Kilroy-Silk! pass gently by!

JAMES FENTON
New Statesman, 1977

This was, I think, the first time Michael Heseltine hypnotised the Tory conference with a speech. As one of his colleagues remarked to me on this occasion, 'Michael knows exactly where to find the clitoris of the Conservative party.'

Hair apparent

There will soon be a new word in the language; to heseltine, meaning to build up a monumental pile of blonde hair, fix it in place with a complicated system of scaffolding and webs, and then spray it with lacquer. It would be advertised in hairdressers': 'Unisex shampoo and heseltine, £3.'

Young men would have their hair specially heseltined for their first speech at a Tory conference. Mrs Thatcher has hers heseltined every week. Unfortunately, something has gone wrong with the display mounted on the original owner.

Mr Michael Heseltine is the Environment spokesman, and by now probably the most popular single figure for the Tory faithful. Yesterday he was supposed to be talking about local government but this got only a short look in as he produced instead a mighty anti-Socialist diatribe designed, no doubt, to show what a great Tory leader he will make.

It was being said that he had been put into the slot just before lunch in order to punish him for being so overwhelmingly popular last year. The idea was that if he overran the delegates would get angry about missing their lunch and he would be driven from the platform by the concerted rumbling of tummies. In the event they loved it so much that he could have gone right through lunch-time, dinner, and into breakfast this morning.

But to the detached observer the fascination lay in the terrible things that were happening to his hair. Something had gone dreadfully wrong with the engineering system holding it up. Great chunks of it crashed down, like cliffs falling into the sea, covering his forehead and sometimes blotting out his eyes.

Now and again he tried to shore it up in mid-speech, but then a bit would sheer off and crash around his ears. By the end the whole noble edifice was in ruins, a sad reminder of the frailty of man-made things.

What makes him so popular is, I think, the air of controlled lunacy. He manages to appear as if he is so outraged by Socialism and by the present Government that it is only by supreme self-control that he can prevent himself from picking up the lectern and smashing it on to the nearest Socialist. . . .

Sometimes he even loses touch with his voice and weird involuntary squeaks creep in at the top of his vocal register. All in all, it is amazingly effective, and it is no wonder that they stopped the conference ball to applaud him when he walked in last year.

One young man who had obviously had his hair heseltined for the day was a 16-year-old from the Rother Valley called William Hague. One hesitates to say too much about the young men at

this Tory conference, except that there are an awful lot of them and they are terrifyingly confident. Young William had a surprisingly elderly-sounding Yorkshire accent which made his voice sound almost exactly like Harold Wilson's, to the obvious confusion of delegates who had their backs turned. He had, however, a far greater command of the cliché than the former Prime Minister, and he marked the economic debate with phrases like 'rolling back the frontiers of the state', 'home-owning democracy', 'large and progressive cuts in public spending', and 'a society where effort and initiative are rewarded'. The sight of these aged saws coming from so young a head had the entire conference on its feet at the end of his speech.

The most disconcerting thing of all was that William did not even look surprised as Mrs Thatcher herself leant over from the platform to applaud him. He merely seemed faintly pleased, as if he had won the hundred-yard dash or the school prize for diligence.

SIMON HOGGART
The Guardian, 1977

In 1976 the Confederation of British Industry decided that it should hold an annual conference, like the TUC. I found it remarkably dull, and was delighted by the way Fenton skilfully wove a richly entertaining column from the dross.

Wind and Fire

The meteorological chart looked like a walnut whirl. When the isobars are so close together, it was explained, the inevitable consequence is wind. And wind there was. At Morecambe it put an end to the pier. Throughout the North West there were floods and destruction. In Brighton it was rather less dramatic, but there were moments when I wondered whether the CBI might not be picked up by a gust, whirled around over the city and flung unceremonially into the finny deep. 'Wondered' is perhaps the wrong word. 'Fervently hoped' is more like it.

This was the CBI's first conference – a vast and lavish affair. There were 1,200 delegates, nearly all of them male. About eight miles of suiting material, a total inside leg measurement of at least 1,000 yards, 2,400 sock suspenders crammed into one room! Who could fail to be impressed? They had decided that it was time the public really heard their case. Let the message go forth, they said, from this great conference of ours . . . And what was the message? The message was: on the one hand, it is absolutely vital that our employees do not get paid too much; on the other hand, it is absolutely essential that *we* get a great deal more money ourselves. We're skint, broke, short of the necessary. Give us the moolah, they said, and give us lots of it, now, chop-chop. It was totally unfair, they said, that income should ever be taxed at more than 50 per cent. It was, as one of them beautifully expressed it, *psychologically wrong*. They were fed up with being merely rich. It would be psychologically more appropriate, they felt, to be stinkers. Well, *psychologically*, it would be much better for everybody if they were, shall we say, squillionaires, with an 'investment income' (we aren't supposed to use the term 'unearned income') of ten million shmillion greenies a week, and no questions asked. After listening to this message for a day, I felt it psychologically right to return to London.

JAMES FENTON
New Statesman, 1977

Most Gallery writers in Parliament are not members of the Lobby, the restricted and secretive group of political correspondents who have personal access to MPs and ministers on condition that they never quote them directly. Fenton was a member, and wrote some of the sharpest attacks on the system. He also invented his own lobby rules: lies and insults, he announced, were always on the record. His humorous approach was, I think, more effective than the pompous outrage with which the lobby is usually denounced.

Common Sense about Lobbies

'Now, let me introduce you to an MP,' said my colleague, showing me round Annie's Bar for the first time. He found one. We shook hands and were about to exchange civilities when something rather peculiar happened to the MP. He began to list – first sideways, then backwards, then sideways again. Then his bar-stool proved inadequate, and he fell slowly to the ground. It seemed to take him ages to fall. It was like a slow-motion shoot-out in a late Sixties film. When he had finally achieved the carpet he was picked up and helped to his room. I thought to myself: 'I'm not seeing this. I must not "see" anything in the private rooms and corridors of the Palace of Westminster. I am a guest of Parliament, and it has always been the rule that incidents, pleasant or otherwise, should be treated as private if they happen in those parts of the building to which I have access because my name is on the Lobby List. This rule is strictly enforced by the authorities. This rule is strictly . . .' 'I think we had better find someone else to talk to,' said my colleague.

The Lobby Rules have always held a certain charm for me: 'Do not run after a Minister or Private Member. It is nearly always possible to place oneself in a position to avoid this.' Presumably in the bad old days, whenever there was a sighting of an important Minister, a cry of 'View Halloo!' went up, and the whole pack of lobbymen went racing down the Ways and Means. The rule was no doubt introduced to protect such elder statesmen as had become a little shaky on their pins. Another rule: 'Do not crowd together in the Lobby so as to be conspicuous.' And: 'Do not crowd round the Vote Office when an important document is expected.' So serious a Lobby correspondent was I that every time an important document was expected I made myself scarce.

But the most interesting feature of the rules was epistemological. The Oxford philosophers used to say that a statement was meaningful if it was susceptible of proof. The Lobby Rules, on the other hand, are ingeniously designed to ensure that no statement will be susceptible of proof. A policeman in court is encouraged to read from his notebook. But the lobbyman is told: 'Do not use a notebook, or, as a rule, make notes when in private conversation, in the Members' Lobby.' All journalists are supposed where necessary to protect their sources, but the lobbyman is supposed to make this his 'primary duty':

> Sometimes it may be right to protect your informant to the extent of not using a story at all. This has often been done in the past, and it forms one of the foundations of the good and confidential relationship between the Lobby and members of all parties.

'Good afternoon, Minister. Any good stories today?' 'Matter of fact, yes, we're going to war. But keep it under your hat, what?' 'Come, come, Minister, when have I ever used a story you gave me? Silent as the grave, that's my motto!' 'Well, I know. You're a credit to your paper, Fentiman. I don't think I've seen any story under your by-line for the last six months. I say, you haven't seen the PM around have you? There's an urgent message for him from the chiefs of staff.' 'Ho, ho, ho. You can't catch me out like that, minister. Do you think I "see" anything that goes on here . . .?' (North Korean storm-troopers sweep through the Lobby, chopping up members of all parties, disembowelling the sergeant-at-arms, crowding round the Vote Office.) '. . . pleasant or otherwise?' 'For Christ sake Fentiman, we've got to get out of here double quick. Follow me.' (Minister runs off down Ways and Means.) Fentiman: 'Ho, ho, ho. Trying to catch me out again. Imagine what the Lobby Committee would have to say if I was caught running after a Minister in the w- AARGH!'

This, at any rate, is the way the Lobby is supposed to work. The most distinctive feature of the system, I suppose, is the regular meetings held in the special lobby room in which Mrs Thatcher, Michael Foot and Tom McCaffrey brief the press on the current state of play. The fact that these meetings are held is supposed to be kept secret:

> Do not talk about Lobby meetings BEFORE or AFTER they are held, especially in the presence of those not entitled to attend them. If outsiders appear to know something of the arrangements made by the Lobby, do not confirm their conjectures, or

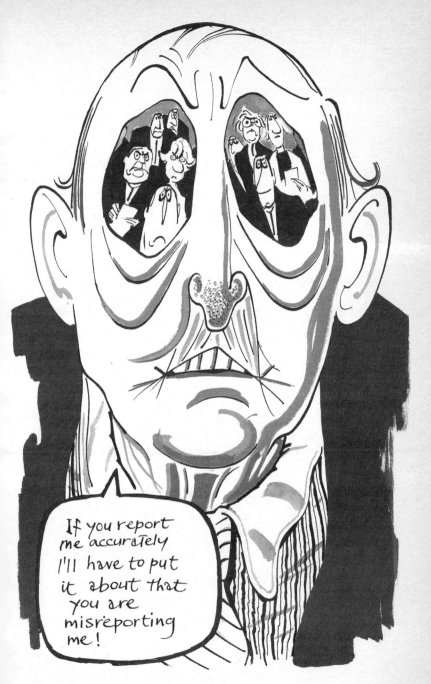

assume that, as they appear to know so much, they may safely be told the rest.

The wording of this rule makes it sound as if the lobbymen are made privy to the most extraordinary range of secrets. In fact, the only use of the system is to enable those who give the briefings to deny accurate press accounts of what they have said.

JAMES FENTON
New Statesman, 1978

Willie Whitelaw was one of the most popular MPs among both Lobby correspondents and Gallery writers. He was best known for 'Willieisms', absurd non-sequiturs which nevertheless were perfectly easy to understand. 'It is a great mistake ever to pre-judge the past,' he once said. In 1974 he accused the Labour government of 'going around the country stirring up complacency'. When I met him in Barrow during the 1979 election, he said cheerfully: 'I expect you've come to hear some of my famous remarks.'

Willie whirls in with whiffs of grapeshot

Mr William Whitelaw, the Tory deputy leader, descended like a tornado on the North-west yesterday.

Mr Whitelaw meets the electorate in the way a combine harvester meets a field of wheat, with impressive, even ruthless efficiency. 'Hello, how nice to meet you, how very nice to meet you, thank you so much, very good to meet you, thank you so very much,' he will say to a single voter.

Show him a group of shoppers and he is among them, scattering greetings and hand-shakes like grapeshot. 'Very nice to meet you, very kind of you, so nice to see you!' While greeting one group he might spot another moving out of range a few yards away. But there is no escape. 'How are you? Oh good! Very nice to meet you!'

A team of Tory campaigners is sent on ahead to line up people to be introduced. Feeding the Leviathan is a full-time job and sometimes they accidentally catch journalists, Mr Whitelaw's detectives, and each other – anyone to gorge the endless appetite.

Now and again he bursts suddenly into a shop and rains greetings on half a dozen customers and assistants in less than five seconds. 'Marvellous to meet you! Very kind! Very good to see you!'

One longed for someone to clutch his sleeve and say: 'But you don't know me, Mr Whitelaw! How can you know the real me, my hopes, my fears, my secret dreams?' But of course no one did.

A few stopped to discuss politics and they all got a straight answer, even if it risked votes. 'I wouldn't vote for me on that basis, because I don't believe it,' he told one woman.

Almost everyone recognises him and looks pleased to see him and only a handful declined to meet him. One teenager said: 'I am not into that kind of thing, man.' At full tilt he can meet the voters at the rate of 13 a minute, more than 700 an hour, quite enough to swing a marginal seat.

In Barrow, the first of 12 engagements in the day, he attracted crowds of old ladies who wanted to kiss and cuddle him. Many were lucky. One tried to kiss him twice. 'You mustn't do that, they'll talk about us,' he said. Some were so smitten that they hung round and were introduced two or three times.

We descended on Tesco's where the pickings were sparse – no more than half a dozen people to be greeted at the dairy produce counter, but the dotty ladies were in wait at the checkout. One of them gave him a playful but painful looking slap on the face. Another said slyly: 'I have already met you.'

'Lovely, marvellous, very good to meet you again!' To a woman who walked backwards waving a Liberal poster: 'Well, if you want to vote that way you will have to make up your own mind!'

Some of the old ladies were worried about law and order, but he flatly refuses any talk of hanging and flogging. 'Most important to boost police morale, mistake to change the law too quickly, thank you so much, very good to have met you.'

Willie whirls in.

His ebullience disappears only when Ulster is raised, which it is surprisingly often. One old lady said: 'I hope you'll do something for Northern Ireland.' And he answered, sadly: 'Well, I did try, didn't I? I had such hopes when I was there, and I can never get quite away from my feelings about it.'

One supporter said: 'Your party leader is losing votes,' and he said: 'No. I don't think so, I really can't accept that.' Mr Whitelaw was always the ultimate loyalist, making faithful dog Tray look like Benedict Arnold.

SIMON HOGGART
The Guardian, 1979

Mrs Thatcher's image-maker was Gordon Reece, who realised that in a TV age, it was powerful visual images which mattered. In 1979 he made it his business to arrange them. This was really the first full TV election in Britain.

Mrs Thatcher continued to travel around the country telling everyone she met that a Conservative Government would be all right. On a more serious note, she also ran amok in a Birmingham chocolate factory. For those of us who have been on the trail with her this was indisputably the big event so far.

Finding herself by chance in the extremely marginal constituency of Selly Oak – Labour majority 326 – she decided to call in on the voters on the Cadbury assembly line who bring you your walnut fudge in soft caramel, hazel crispy cluster and bitter lemon crunch, and who are therefore responsible probably for more coronaries than anyone in Britain apart from the pro-jogging lobby. It was a discreet visit – just the Leader of the Opposition and about a hundred television and Press photographers and reporters.

Before we were disgorged into the factory we all had to put on white coats and hats to make us hygienic. We then advanced on the unsuspecting folk on the conveyor belts. The famous factory is as superbly organised as legend has it, but is rather noisy.

67

Apparently the manufacture of chocolates is a process which makes a noise like Niagara Falls. Into this existing uproar erupted Mrs Thatcher pursued by a hundred white coats. The whole effect resembled perhaps a lunatic asylum in which the doctors had themselves gone berserk; or possibly a convention of mad surgeons.

The entire surrealist canvas was the most picturesque which your correspondent has witnessed in a decade or so of observing politicians trying to become Prime Minister. Mrs Thatcher would descend on a chocolate woman (that is to say a woman making chocolate). They would have a conversation. Because of the din, neither could hear the other. This is the ideal arrangement for conversations between party leaders and voters at election time since it cuts out a lot of unnecessary detail.

Meanwhile, Mr Denis Thatcher, the husband, would lurk on the fringe of the affray conversing with employees who did not quite get to talk to his wife. He has developed an impressive line in Duke of Edinburgh factory visit chat. It goes something like: 'This is the assortments section, I gather . . . interesting . . . Do you export much? . . . Really? Africa as well . . . but surely it would melt?'

Back at base, the Leader of the Opposition would inevitably be urged to try chocolate packing herself. The problem, of course, would have been to stop her. Maniacally, she would raid the hazel crispy clusters and shove them in passing boxes. At this, those of the deranged doctors who had cameras would ecstatically close in with their tripods, lights and, in the case of the TV men, those strange objects which look like small bazookas and are to do with the sound. Some of them would clamber on chairs and machines to get a better angle. Thus clustered together at many different levels, they became not just mad surgeons but mad Martian surgeons as a result of their extra, deformed electronic eyes and cables coming out of their heads. In the midst of the tiers of lenses and faces the visage of the occasional Japanese photographer or correspondent would peer out framed perhaps by huge piles of Bournville selection. This was an extra loony touch.

What a scene! The genius at Conservative Central Office who thought it up must get a knighthood.

In the middle of it all the little chocolate woman who was the object of Mrs Thatcher's rapt attention would rather tend to get forgotten. Eventually we would all move further on down the conveyor belt or up to the next floor, the entire progress taking place before the disbelieving gaze of the Cadbury's employees on the conveyor belts. The squeals were understandable. It was exciting for me. It must have been mindblowing for folk who have to sit all day transferring the plain-coated nougat into the boxes of 'Contrast'. From department to department there was no abating of the noise. Squeals! roaring machinery! and Denis still doing his stuff: 'Fascinating . . . but how do you get the walnut exactly in the middle of the fudge?'

It was occasionally hazardous for those of us caught up in the heavy, swaying throng. Machines bubbled and clattered within inches. The Leader of the Conservative Party, borne irresistibly on by the deranged mob, was herself at times fortunate not to be converted into a large mass of delicious hazel crispy cluster.

Next week, with luck, a cement factory!

FRANK JOHNSON
The Times, 1979

In 1981, after terrible rioting in Toxteth, Michael Heseltine was appointed by Mrs Thatcher to look into the problems of Merseyside. In spite of some sniggering at Westminster, he set about the job with a will.

For over seven days and nights now, Mr Michael Heseltine has been running amok all over Merseyside. At his temporary office in the Royal Liver Building, they said he was to be found at the community centre at Skelmersdale. At Skelmersdale, they said he had been there but had just left for Runcorn. At Runcorn I asked a policeman where Mr Heseltine was. 'Who was he?' this constable gratifyingly replied. Some years on the political trail have taught me that one of the great strengths of British democracy is that there are always pockets of ignorance about even the most self-publicising of our rulers.

One explained to the policeman that Mr Heseltine was the new Minister for places like Merseyside and that sort of thing. You could not miss him. He was about seven foot tall, with what looked like a blond wig but was, so far as we knew, real hair. This man was believed to be in the area. 'The public have been warned not to approach him, but to call the police instead.' I said, adding a tentative 'Ha, ha, ha.'

The constable looked bleak. Never try to be funny with policemen, one's auntie used to say. The policeman radioed headquarters: 'I've got a fella 'ere who says he's a reporter and he's looking for Mr Heseltine, who's the Minister of Merseyside. He's about seven foot tall and he's got blond hair that looks like a wig . . . no, not the reporter, the Minister.'

Someone at headquarters told the policeman to turn down his radio, presumably so that I could not hear what was being said. After a conversation, the constable explained: 'No, we don't know where he is.' It seemed clear that the forces of law and order knew of his whereabouts, but assumed, as authority always does, that Ministers do not want to be bothered by their subjects.

Parting from the constable, I explained that Mr Heseltine had been sent up after the riots. 'I blame the parents,' said the policeman. 'Oh, I don't think old Heseltine's parents are to blame for the way he's turned out,' I replied. The policeman stared. It was time to be off.

'Perhaps Mr Heseltine doesn't want any publicity,' said another constable later. Mr Heseltine not wanting any publicity! As soon argue that Dracula did not want any blood. None the less, it was time to retire to the hotel and bed. But there, the following morning, in the lobby, encased in 7 ft of Savile Row suiting and 4 ft of Jermyn Street shirting, awash in half a gallon of after-shave, was Mr Heseltine. He was roaring off to a couple of job-training centres. It was not, of course, entirely true that he was avoiding publicity, but there was some truth in it.

Becoming an 'emergency' or 'crisis' or 'special' minister is a perilous adventure for a politician. Everybody says it is a gimmick and, in any case, too little too late. Afterwards, when nothing much happens which would not have happened in any case, he gets blamed. Also, people are apt to laugh at him and ask questions like: 'Who needs a riot when you've got Michael Heseltine?' Look at Lord Hailsham on the North-East, Mr Denis Howell on the drought.

The assignment does have its good side. He gets in the papers and on television a lot. But the publicity is difficult to control. He gets pictured going importantly in and out of meetings, staring at slums with a look of concern, and he gives interviews in which he can say statesmanlike things such as that there are no easy solutions, and that he is at present here to listen.

But it is difficult to control what is said at all these meetings if there are difficult people there.

Terence Moore, of Caryl Gardens – which are no gardens but an unrelenting block of flats – was waiting for him with a few inmates, being rather cynical. 'Tarzan, they call him,' Mr Moore explained. 'So they should tell him to plant some trees around this place.' Terence's brother, Albert, said his wife had read out from that morning's *Mirror* where it said Mr Heseltine had spent £10,000 over the weekend on his daughter's birthday party – £10,000 quid, Albert emphasised. It would have been better spent getting the fungus off these walls.

The suit containing the crisis minister turned up. Terence waylaid him. 'Why wasn't Mr Heseltine meeting the people here in the houses they had to live in?' Mr Heseltine replied that he had gone into some houses yesterday. 'He's got three houses himself,' I whispered to Terence's brother, Albert, hoping to make the full and frank exchanges still more constructive. 'You've got three houses yourself,' said Albert, 'I saw it in the papers.' But Mr Heseltine was still engaged with Terence.

'My job is to see as many things as possible. I think I've got a picture of the housing problem . . .' We hurried off to an employment exchange, or a 'job centre', in the Old Swan district.

Lured by the television cameras, a small crowd had gathered. A Mrs Durant, of Alston Street, approached me to ask whether this Mr Heseltine was worried about employment. If so, her husband had a scrapyard, but they were making him close it down because they wanted the land for trees. 'They don't need trees around there,' she said, 'they just break them down to hit each other with.' (Terence's complaint, if you remember, was the precise opposite. He wanted *more* trees. The public, you see, can not agree on these matters.) I urged her to raise the problem with Mr Heseltine, who would be here in a moment.

'Do you think I should?' she said. Certainly. He would be very interested. The suit entered, suffused in television lighting, and was escorted forward by the manager. Fortunately, Mrs Durant managed to nip in. 'Mr Heseltine,' she said. 'You're here about jobs. Well, my husband's got a scrapyard but they want it for trees and . . .'

Mr Heseltine thanked her and said he couldn't deal with that now and turned her in the direction of 'one of my officials'. A luckless official was right behind. Mrs Durant got going again. He produced a pen and a notebook. 'I'll follow it up with the city,' he could be heard saying, 'I can't promise anything. Scrapyards *are* unpopular . . .'

FRANK JOHNSON
The Times, 1981

A Mr William Pitt, of the SDP/Liberal Alliance, as it was known in those distant days, won the Croydon by-election. Johnson's column includes one of the rare public attacks on Lord Goodman, the celebrated lawyer. There was a general attitude in newspaper offices at the time that to poke fun at politicians was all very well, but that Lord Goodman was a national monument, like the Queen, or Nelson's column, and thus immune from jocularity. Pitt lost the seat at the subsequent general election.

Something interesting has happened at last.

Not Lord Goodman himself could find a smear worthy of the name in this unhealthily polite contest, one had mused in the comatose depths of the constituency the other day. But one should not take the Lord's name in vain. For one thing, to do so tends to cost thousands. Yesterday, in its closing hours, there came an unscheduled guest appearance from the face that launched a thousand writs, the man who put the junk in injunction, the greatest

73

solicitor since Cicero: Lord Goodman. Two housewives had allegedly made certain remarks to two Liberal canvassers about Mr William Pitt, the Liberal/SDP Alliance candidate, in his capacity as chairman of a local residents' association. Whereupon, astoundingly, both women received through their letterboxes a terrifying letter from Messrs Goodman Derrick and Co – a letter of the kind that Lord Goodman has unleashed to bludgeon mighty newspapers and giant corporations down the ages.

The document's existence was discovered by the Labour Party which yesterday reproduced it in 5,000 leaflets warning voters, immortally, that if you tell Mr Pitt to get lost you might receive a letter from Lord Goodman. The pamphlet ends triumphantly: 'Stan Boden, your local Labour candidate, doesn't need a top people's lawyer. His door (47, Eversly Road) will always be open – whether you want to deliver bouquets or brickbats.' The pamphlet omits to mention that Lord Goodman, as public figure, was largely invented by the Labour Party. But no matter. At this stage, we must proceed warily. For at the name of Goodman every pen shall cower. It must be emphasised that everyone mentioned from now on is a person of unblemished reputation, total integrity, and personal freshness, except if Messrs Goodman Derrick and Co say they are not. Furthermore, there is not a jot or tittle of evidence for any suggestion to the contrary – or jit or tottle, tittle or bottle. There is not a scintilla, whatever that may mean, of any other evidence. It is all a farrago of untruths, and indeed, a fandango if required. (Lord Goodman's prose style is infectious on these occasions.) The letter demonstrates once again that Lord Goodman has no peer as an exponent of the legal-pomposo school of English.

'Dear Madam,' it begins. (A little impersonal, that, but it is probable that, just as with a Bellini or a Veronese, not all of the letter comes from the hand of the master himself, but from lesser members of the School of Goodman. That opening may have been the work of Derrick.) 'We act on behalf of Mr William Pitt,' the document continues. (All his life, the history-conscious Lord Goodman has regretted that he has never been able to write that sentence. Another ambition achieved.) 'It has been drawn to our attention that on the 17th October you made certain allega-

Lord Goodman coming down heavily.

tions . . .' Some of the phrases are rather dead, admittedly. More work by Derrick, one suspects. At this point a colleague has reminded me that Derrick is dead. That would explain it. None the less, experts would agree that the work is still priceless. For one after another the familiar phrases roll out. 'Our client strongly refutes these allegations . . . without prejudice to our client's rights . . . in respect of allegations already made, we are instructed to inform you . . . proceedings . . . forthwith . . .' It is all there. A masterpiece, albeit a minor one. The work ends with a tremendous, overwhelming, life-enhancing: '. . . including, if necessary, injunction proceedings to prevent you from repeating these allegations.'

Asked to comment yesterday, one of the recipients, Mrs Joyce Adams, understandably observed: 'When it arrived I couldn't believe It.' But she added. 'I'm not frightened,' which is more than can be said of the present writer. None the less, one will hazard the protest that things have come to a sad pass when you cannot slander a by-election candidate to a couple of his canvassers without there thudding through your letterbox a missive from the most numbing notary in the history of the British legal system.

FRANK JOHNSON
The Times, 1981

The Socialist Royal Family was one of Wharton's best running gags.

Norman the Good

There were angry scenes in Parliament yesterday when Trev Nobes, One-party member for Windermere New Town, asked the Home Secretary, One-party member Jim Binns, what steps the Royal Socialist Household was taking to cut down expenses in the present economic crisis.

Replying, the Home Secretary said that Mrs J. Smith, the Royal Socialist Domestic Help in the Council Palace, had up to the end of last year worked there four days a week for six hour periods, with three statutory tea-breaks. Her work had now been cut to four hour periods two days a week, with five statutory tea-breaks.

Member Nobes: Is there any reason why the Socialist Royal Family should employ any domestic help whatever? The practice is degrading both for the Socialist Royal Family itself, which should by this time have shed all such relics of feudalism, and for Mrs Smith, who has recently contributed an article, 'My Days as a Royal Socialist Serf', to the *Sunday Defective* which contains astonishing revelations of this survival of the bad old days.

Member Frank Tilt (Oxbrum Conurbation, Banbury Division): Has Member Nobes seen a rejoinder from HRSM the Queen Gran in the same newspaper, claiming that Mrs Smith never did a hand's turn but sat about drinking tea and eating up the Royal Socialist supply of austerity ginger biscuits (16 pts) while she (HRSM the Queen Gran) and HRSM Queen Doreen, whose washing machine had been broken by careless handling, took turns at the mangle? (uproar; shouts of 'Suez!' 'Boycott South Africa!' 'Yanks out of North America!' etc, etc.)

Member Nobes: Has Member Tilt read Mr Smith's account of how HRSM the Queen Gran threatened to put her (Mrs Smith) through the mangle? (uproar).

Member Tilt: I am not pleading for the retention of domestic help for the Royal Socialist Household. On the contrary, I am drawing attention to the brutal facts, in the hope that this mediaeval custom, more suited to the tapestried courts of Louis XIV or the pillared halls of the tyrant Nero than to a Royal Socialist Council Palace, may be abolished altogether (applause, uproar etc.).

PETER SIMPLE
The Daily Telegraph, 1981

Another regrettable attack on Roy Hattersley, who is unable to answer for himself.

Parallels

J. W. Goethe, an Eighteenth Century Roy Hattersley (£4.75, paper-

back £1.95) is the latest in Viper and Bugloss's excellent 'Parallels' series, which includes *Jean Racine: a French Arnold Wesker* and *Dante Alighieri: an Italian Harold Pinter.*

The aim of the series is to introduce obscure writers of the past and show how they anticipated aspects of the work of the giants of today.

Johann Wolfgang von Goethe, who seems to have lived until 1832 (curiously enough – can it have been a psychic premonition? – he is said to have given himself the nickname 'Roy' as a child, though it was afterwards dropped) was a German poet, essayist, amateur scientist and social reformer who also played a part in local politics.

It is fascinating to note how this almost forgotten minor figure, who dabbled, in his limited way, in so many fields of activity from the literary to the political, shadowed forth in miniature the achievements of our own great English writer-statesman.

PETER SIMPLE
The Daily Telegraph, 1982

Roy Jenkins won Glasgow Hillhead after the by-election campaign which Johnson visited. At the time this looked like a tremendous break-through for the new Social Democratic Party. Jenkins held the seat until the 1987 general election.

To Hillhead, to take in the by-election campaign. It is good to see it before it finishes. Any visitor getting into any fashionable by-election before the end of its run knows just enough about it to make it confusing . . .

Suddenly, there was a twist. Over the weekend the polls moved in Mr Jenkins's favour. A telephone poll put him ahead while the latest, in the *Daily Express*, had the Tory less than one per cent in front – in effect a dead heat. Mr Jenkins could bloom again. He was not listless now.

'I never comment on polls,' he told us. But purely by chance he detected 'a movement' in his favour. That word 'movement' was drawn out to prodigious lengths – as if summoned up from the deepest recesses of his cultured tonsils – m-u-u-r-v-m-o-n-t – and accompanied by that shaking of the jowl and authoritative gesture with the hand indicating some gathering, unstoppable force of history.

The true Mr Jenkins was among us again. He was back on form – this much-loved, gracious figure who is to the liberal classes what the Queen Mother is to the rest of us. What evidence had he for the muurvmont, if it was not those polls about which he never commented? That presented him with a problem, but not for long. He stared upwards and called up an answer. I was so transfixed by it, having attended performances by Mr Jenkins since childhood, that I took it down afterwards from a colleague's tape recorder so as to provide the literary world with the authentic, unchallengeable text.

'What struck me very much was the spontaneity of the response in the shopping centres in all parts of the constituency,' began this dignified figure from whom Scottish shoppers have apparently been fleeing in awe for weeks, 'and the responsive waving primarily when we drove around making our noise.'

Note the magical term 'responsive waving'. People do not just go in for any old wave when Mr Jenkins hits the shopping centres.

They *responsively* wave, 'primarily', as is made clear in the text, when he drives around making his noise. What noise, the philistine might well inquire? It cannot be his muurvmonts. They would not be enough to get him a good round of responsive waves; quite the opposite. Inquiries later elicited the clarification that 'our noise' was the splendidly disdainful way in which the candidate referred to the SDP's theme tune, Aaron Copland's *Fanfare for the Common Man*. The common man referred to in this context, it should be explained, is not Mr Jenkins. Quite the opposite. It is he who is the fanfare.

In these final days of the by-election campaign, the energy problem has emerged as a key issue.

Mr Roy Jenkins regards his energy as a precious national asset that must be conserved. His Labour opponents are demanding to know how much of it, if elected tomorrow, he would be prepared to expend on Hillhead. The issue came to the fore as follows:

Mr Roy Hattersley, the Shadow Home Secretary, arrived on Monday and, addressing a factory gate meeting, reminded people that Mr Jenkins had represented a neighbouring constituency to his in Birmingham. Mr Hattersley implied that during those years Mr Jenkins had always taken care to husband his resources. But by yesterday's Labour press conference, the party was warning Hillhead of a massive lethargy crisis if Mr Jenkins won.

The issue, then, was whether, if elected, supplies of Mr Jenkins in Hillhead would soon run out? To the independent analyst, there seemed every possibility that this might happen. The more interesting question was: did the voters much mind if it did?

The evidence suggested that the voters were rather less priggish and high minded about the matter than the politicians. It was announced that Mr Jenkins, protruding through the open roof of a motor vehicle, would be drawn in some pomp around the constituency yesterday in a motorcade escorted by a detachment of halbardiers and pikemen up from the crack moderate regiments of London. Here was a chance to see whether Hillhead shared Labour's doubts about Mr Jenkins's devotion to them, and whether he was as ill-at-ease among the Scots as earlier reports would have it.

Well, it can be reported now that Mr Jenkins's state visit to several shopping centres occasioned scenes of widespread responsive waving. Every now and then he would stop and walk among the people. There was little hostility. What socialists never understand is that the citizenry has nothing against the traditional hereditary ruling class as such. To this it may be replied that Mr Jenkins is not a traditional hereditary ruler. But it is too late to start confusing people . . .

When working the shopping centre pavements, Mr Jenkins, once he had trained his woman in his sights, would approach her, and engage her in fatuously polite conversation, bowing slightly from the waist, and sometimes making a graceful gesture as if to raise his hat to her, a considerable trick considering that he was not wearing a hat at the time.

This last gesture would consist of simultaneously raising the hand and lowering the head. And what a head! An egghead, certainly, but a Fabergé of an egghead – shining, exquisitely crafted, full of delights.

'I'm a dyed-in-the-wool Tory, but he's a marvellous man,' Mrs Margaret Graham, of Churchill Drive, replied when I asked her for her opinion just after he had worked her over. She added: 'He has held some of the most important jobs, and he has deported himself in them very well.' How Mr Jenkins would have approved of the idea that he 'deported' himself. For that indeed is what he does . . .

It has been, by all accounts, a joyous campaign and it is no disservice to the other principal candidates to say that this is because of the presence of Mr Roy Jenkins.

Mr Malone, the Tory, some thirty years Mr Jenkins's junior, manifestly has more knowledge of 'the issues', including the national ones, than Mr Jenkins, with weary decades of issues stretching back behind him, can nowadays muster. But somehow, it is right that Mr Malone should know the details that Mr Jenkins should not. For this is Jenkins: the Last Phase; the period when the finished man is known to us all and we judge him by what he would *be* in office rather than what he would do, which is in the case of any politician largely unknowable in any case. Nothing would go exceptionally right under Mr Jenkins's rule. But nothing would go exceptionally wrong, either, and it would all be done with some aplomb.

The Hillhead voters sense this, which is why, though his opponents have convincingly demonstrated over the past week that his attitude on the issues is indistinct, his rise in the opinion polls has gathered momentum.

Perhaps the voters are tired of issues. And politicians are to be enjoyed for other reasons. There is what might be called, for want of a better term, their carry-on; the props, gestures and mild absurdities which make them stand out from lesser, greyer, figures.

When Mr Jenkins is carrying on, the tone is raised, the atmosphere is sweeter. That is why this by-election, whether he wins or loses it, has been a success. Our attitude to Mr Jenkins is very similar to that of the old ladies of Hillhead. We just like to hear him talk.

Yesterday was the traditional eve of poll rally of clichés, the day when all candidates detect a 'late swing', or 'scent victory' or are 'quietly confident'.

Such phrases are of course quite separate from the Royisms which give us so much pleasure. But we none the less like to hear them from Mr Jenkins's cultured tones and distinguished, quivering jowls because from such a source they sound as new. The interest of his final press conference, then, lay in seeing how many we could coax from him.

As soon as he arrived, we knew he was going to carry on. 'My reaction in shopping centres, in what I would regard as nodal areas of the constituency, has been very striking,' he drawled. Nodal areas? So he could still produce a new Royism on the last day.

Later research in a dictionary revealed that 'nodals' were 'great circles of the celestial sphere, especially the orbit of a planet or the moon'. There were few of those in Hillhead, so we opted for the secondary meaning: a meeting-place of roads, unless he meant, with that distinctive voice of his, noodle areas, a reference to Hillhead's hitherto unnoticed Chinatown. It did not really matter.

'There is every sign of a substantial movement of opinion which has gone on and is going on, a real late swing.'

'At Crosby, you said you scented victory,' asked a colleague from the BBC, choosing the cliché that would give Mr Jenkins almost the full set. 'At Crosby, I said that, did I? Yes, I've been scenting victory for some time in this campaign,' he replied.

'We're not cocky, but we're quietly confident,' he added, achieving the full set. Whereupon, Mr Jenkins ended the press conference which could have been the last of his electoral career or the herald to that career's apotheosis.

But the memory of his campaign which lingers most was his reply to a persistent young man in a menacing leather jacket who had upbraided him in a nodal area about leaving the Labour Party. 'I believe in a fair society, which we will govern far more

effectively than an extremist Marxist Labour Party, and goodbye.'
That was Mr Roy Jenkins's election address to the voters of Hillhead.

FRANK JOHNSON
The Times, 1982

The Argentine invasion of the Falklands led to that most unusual of
parliamentary occasions – a Saturday sitting. The nation sat glued to its
radios. As Bernard Levin pointed out 25 years earlier, when the House of
Commons thinks it is at its best, it is generally at its worst.

A Majority for Blood

In its fury yesterday, the House of Commons turned on a discredited, tinpot Government which, in order to divert attention
from its crippling domestic problems, has got itself engaged in a
foreign imbroglio.

MPs also had some harsh words for the Argentine junta. But
there was no doubt where they expected to see the first blood
spilled – on the Conservative front bench. At this darkest hour of
his career the Defence Secretary, Mr John Nott, behaved as we
have come to expect all the great politicians to behave – he made
an ass of himself.

The House was packed for the first Saturday sitting since Suez
in 1956. Outside the public gallery there were long queues, longer
than had been seen in London since, well, since the first night of
Evita.

Inside the mood was bellicose. This was particularly true on
the Labour benches. One half expected to see Mr Michael Foot
handing out white feathers, or old naval hands like Mr Callaghan
crying 'Eat death, Johnny Gaucho!'

Mrs Thatcher began. Friday, she said, had been a day of
'rumour and counter rumour'. This was not strictly true, since
anyone who read the papers or listened to the radio knew exactly
what was happening. The Prime Minister continued: 'Yesterday

morning we sent a telegram . . .' The Labour side erupted in ersatz mirth for the first time. Hadn't they all read last week that British Telecom had stopped telegrams?

She continued to jeers and booing. The Government had not wanted to escalate the dispute, fear of precipitating the events they had wanted to prevent, and so forth. Then she made her big mistake. She introduced a party point.

Exactly the same thing had happened to the Southern Thule in 1976, and the then Government hadn't even told the House until 1978. Labour backbenchers, many of whom until that moment had thought that the Southern Thule was a new disco step, bayed back in disbelief. Mr Ted Rowlands, the Minister then responsible, stood up and pointed out that unlike the Falklands, Southern Thule was 'totally uninhabited with the exception of penguins and a vast amount of bird droppings.'

Mrs Thatcher continued with the logistical problems which would have been involved in doing something about the problem. She sat down to cries of 'resign', which brought a comforting note of sameness and continuity in these disturbing times.

Mr Foot rose. He was later praised by warlike Conservative back-benchers for having 'spoken for England' – the first time this has happened to the white-haired old pacifist. He called for a counter-invasion. 'The Government must prove itself by deeds, because they will not, I believe, do it by words.' He sat down to the biggest cheers he has heard from the Labour Party since he announced in Brighton last year, 'I am an inveterate peace-monger.'

Mr Edward du Cann began by praising the Government. This is usually the sign that he is going to make a scornful attack on it, and so it proved to be. It was 'astounding' that we were so woefully ill-prepared, 'extraordinary' that forces were not already deployed, 'fatuous' that anyone should have thought it could be solved diplomatically.

'We have nothing to lose except our honour. . . . I am quite certain that it is safe in the hands of the Prime Minister,' he finished. That, from the Chairman of the 1922 Committee, was like a jewelled dagger in Mrs Thatcher's back.

Enoch Powell began by making a short speech about Northern

Ireland – which was unusual for him. He generally makes a much longer speech about Northern Ireland, but clearly even he felt the circumstances were special. He appeared to be looking forward, perhaps with relish, to a court martial of the hapless Royal Marines on the islands. He described the 'infamy' to this country. MPs' vocabulary at least was escalating. A huge task force from Roget's *Thesaurus* had been assembled and was even now being deployed.

Sir Nigel Fisher wanted the most extreme measure of all. Argentina should be banned from the World Cup in Spain. Labour MPs took a moment off from laughing at Mr Nott to laugh at that.

David Owen told the House for roughly the four hundred and sixty-seventh time that a similar situation had blown up when he was Foreign Secretary and that he had solved it. The Government said it had no idea what the Argentines would do – yet their intentions had appeared in the *Guardian* (and the *Observer* for that matter) as long ago as February. This seems a shade harsh on Lord Carrington; after all, few people read the foreign pages of the quality papers, and certainly not the Foreign Office.

Dr Owen suggested a blockade of the islands. This was what the House wanted to hear. Was it the former Foreign Secretary's leadership bid? Probably not, because when he sat down Roy Jenkins said loudly, 'Well done, David.'

By this time it was clear that MPs had three enemies in their sights: in descending order, Mr Nott, the Foreign Office, and the Argentines. Everybody spoke for England, except the SNP leader Donald Stewart, who spoke for Scotland. This turned out to be exactly the same. The entire Dreadnought class of Tory MPs, Mr Julian Amery, Sir Bernard Braine and other names familiar from previous wars, were mobilised and put to sea.

It appeared that Mr Nott had left the front bench and had disappeared. At 12.40 Mr Barry Sherman (Lab, Huddersfield) demanded to know where he was. We expected to hear the sharp crack of a pearl-handled revolver any minute as Mr Nott did the decent thing, and shot an underling, but twenty minutes later he was back.

Mr John Silkin, winding up for the Opposition, wanted the

answers to three key questions, otherwise Mr Nott, Lord Carrington and the Prime Minister herself would have to go. 'It was a collective decision of the three most guilty people in this Government. It is these three who are on trial today,' he declared.

Finally Mr Nott rose confidently to speak. His confidence did not last long. He quibbled desperately about exactly what had happened in 1977 when Labour had faced a similar crisis.

Dr Owen scored another hit on the stern by pointing out that if a Defence Secretary didn't understand about negotiating from strength, he had no right to be a Defence Secretary. When Mr Nott announced to jeers that 'no other country would have reacted so fast. We were not unprepared at all', you could see the smoke pouring from his engine room, hear the band playing 'Nearer My God To Thee'.

By this time the Tories were in open despair, burying their heads in their hands, rolling their eyes to heaven, shaking their heads in pity, and all the other over-theatrical gestures favoured on such occasions.

Nothing could save Mr Nott from sinking with all hands except a sudden, thick fog. Miraculously, this came with the end of the debate at 2 pm prompt.

SIMON HOGGART
The Guardian, 1982

Dennis Skinner, the left-wing MP for Bolsover, thinks of himself as the scourge of the Tories, a vigilante guarding against Labour Party backsliding, and the enemy of prissy Parliamentary rules and conventions. He has however become a victim of the way the House of Commons neutralises its opponents by absorbing them. Skinner is now as much a part of Parliamentary tradition as the Mace and the Speaker's chair.

Beastly time for intrepid Sam in Bolsover

In what may well have been the most reckless gesture of the

general election campaign so far, the Tory candidate for Bolsover yesterday showed his face in Bolsover – on foot and in broad daylight.

The reaction in the sunny Market Square was tremendous. Within minutes a small crowd had begun to form across the street, indicating a strong desire to discuss policy with him.

The cry of 'Vote Skinner' emanated from a couple of ancient throats, soon to be taken up by babes in arms, for whom they are the first words they have been taught.

An old gentleman trundled across to Mr Sam Roberts who is Bolsover Conservatism's choice (from the 39 applicants) to become the latest sacrifice to the voracious political appetite of Mr Dennis Skinner.

'I'm staunch Labour, but I hope your lot get in again,' said the old gent. Mr Roberts brightened. 'I'll tell you why. Because it'll be the end of your Party.' Mr Roberts looked hurt, but then this is his first campaign.

By now the crowd across the street by the butcher's was approaching fifty and growing more confident. Clearly, a sacrifice was needed. Mr Roberts's minder and local chairman, Mr George Webster, a more experienced politician (and 36 years a miner) seemed to be of the opinion that it should be Mr Roberts.

The candidate duly crossed the street and was engulfed by the throng of pensioners, wives, miners on holiday and Labour-voting whippets.

He must have felt like Louis XVI entering Paris or a black suspect entering Alabama. But Mr Skinner's ardent followers were a credit to his continuous programme of political education: articulate, aggressive and outraged but essentially cerebral – and constitutional. No one had brought any rope.

They seemed to know everything, the fall in the value of sterling since 1979, the number of professors sacked at Aston University.

'What about the dual key, then?' asked a woman. 'MacGregor won't even be allowed down the pit at his age,' roared a man.

'And it says in the *Guardian* or the *Observer* that he's in trouble for insider share dealing,' interjected a typical Bolsover voter.

Mr Roberts got in the occasional point above the cries of 'A tin of tomatoes which used to cost 12p now cost 32p' and 'Six-pence to see the doctor, cardboard in our shoes, we remember the thirties all right.'

But he was no match for the electorate. Not quite the usual 'whizzkid from Central Office' trying to take a little shine off Mr Skinner's 18,000 majority, he is 35, a barrister and industrialist from Sheffield, where his father and grandfather were both Tory MPs.

Though what he is doing in Bolsover is basically a Youth Opportunities course in politics.

Being a pleasant enough young man with plenty of cheek but no conspicuous political views, he will probably make it eventually – but not here.

Sam is hanging around for a camera crew from Central TV. So he and his tiny band ('Not Bolsover people,' whispers a respectable Skinnerite) go walkabout, pursued by friendly catcalls.

By the time he gets back to the square a girl from the brass band is playing 'The Red Flag' and Mr Cliff Hawley, President of the Derbyshire miners, is haranguing him with a loud-hailer which he just happens to have in his back pocket.

Sam performs gamely on his own loudhailer for the TV crew. 'I'm Sam Roberts (Boo). Thank you for coming here to support me (Boo) . . . Mr Skinner's majority will be reduced (Boo) by me (So you're not going to win, then).' As I say, Mr Roberts is still learning. 'I feel a bit sorry for him,' admits one of the cerebral tri-coteuses . . .

It is an unexpectedly rural constituency apart from the all-important pits, but Labour controls everything in North Derby-shire. Dark tales are therefore told about the dishing-out of council flats, wardenships and the hushing-up of school arson and attempts to poison the chemistry teacher. It sounds just like Eton.

'Look, a Tory poster in that newsagent's. They're taking a risk,' says Mr Burdett, who is emerging as a sort of Derbyshire Solzhenitsyn.

While Mr Burdett bellows: 'Let's get Dennis out this time,' on the speaker, Sam solicits the vote of a pretty girl who indicates her support for the sitting MP.

'He's done a lot more for me than thou hast fookin' done,' she

shouts as an afterthought. 'Ah, a lady,' mutters Mr Roberts, who
is beginning to get the hang of it.

MICHAEL WHITE
The Guardian, 1983

> Too much writing about Mrs Thatcher has been unthinking praise or
> indiscriminate hatred. Michael White has never made either mistake, and
> his descriptions of her are witty, illuminating and clear-sighted.

Aunt Agatha finds an island realm

As a treat to herself for winning the General Election the Prime
Minister yesterday indulged some of her wilder fantasies: she
routed some hecklers, glanced at some new technology and in-
vaded an island in a hovercraft. The next five years could be like
this.

Quite outstandingly memorable was the last event. The Cowes
estuary on the Isle of Wight may not be San Carlos water but it
is the best thing available within an hour's flight from London.
Round the bend from the helicopter pad came the SRN-6, up
the slipway and into full view. And there she was, standing erect
as any figurehead carved in oak, the nation's chosen leader, supported by an enormous cushion of hot air.

It is moments like this which make the job worth while (hers,
not ours). As she descended to receive the homage of the assembled citizenry she was the personification of Queen Victoria, Elizabeth I, Botticelli's Venus and Jeremy Thorpe in drag. It was all
too much.

Or was it? Was she just another fine flowering of the British
comic genius, in this instance the middle-aged matron on the
rampage: a power-crazed version of Bertie Wooster's Aunt
Agatha? Mrs Thatcher teeters on the edge of self-caricature and
yesterday fell over it several times. It would be a comforting

91

explanation, enabling us all to wake up tomorrow morning and realise that it was all a joke.

In Salisbury market place in the midday heat there is a crowd of 1,000, a quarter of whom support the Labour candidate, who bears the additional burden of being called Lambeth. It is, say media regulars, almost the only real public meeting of the tour. The more they heckle, the more her hackles rise. The hecklers are no match for the hackles. 'Pathetic,' she cries. 'They can only shout because they have not got any arguments left.' The Tories roar.

From Salisbury to the Isle of Wight . . . The candidate seeking to displace the incumbent Liberal, Stephen Ross, is Mrs Virginia Bottomley, whose husband is already a Tory MP. The perfect specimen of an Angela Brazil captain of hockey, she is more Botticelli than Bottomley.

Mrs Thatcher descends from the sky on the British Hovercraft Corporation, which has been starved of government orders and government support, and last year had to lay off 350 workers. The Prime Minister has a cheek to be here at all, but the Prime Minister has a cheek. She makes her triumphant hovercraft landing at the Falcon Yard and inspects the mine-sweeping BII-7 model (briefly) which management and workers plead for – it was beached by Sir John Nott.

A Militant newspaper seller spots Mr Thatcher. 'Hello. Denis,' he begins, before embarking on an unreciprocated discussion of the unfree media with particular reference to the only paper unequivocally to support Labour today, the *Daily Mirror*. 'They won't let you speak on TV because you're an embarrassment, they won't let me speak because I'm dangerous,' he claims.

It is an absurdly British scene. 'Margaret Thatcher, you're a fascist,' roar the Militants two feet from her beloved. Not a fascist, merely mildly authoritarian, mildly magnificent and, let us say, fallible: Aunt Agatha with a clear lead in the opinion polls. Before she leaves for home someone gives her a basket of fresh vegetables. Aunt Agatha is heard to say: 'Don't tip them up, dear. It's best to hold them that way.' Fasten your safety belt.

MICHAEL WHITE
The Guardian, 1983

Richard Needham is another astute Tory MP-cum-writer. His book *Honourable Member* sketches the political career of a young and successful chancer called Pringle Dempster.

By now Pringle Dempster is in his late 20s with a young family and experience in industry and commerce. He is chairman of his local branch and one of the youngest County Councillors and the time has come to apply for a place on the parliamentary candidate's list. No Tory constituency can choose a candidate without Conservative Central Office having first given their approval. Central Office is a daunting and formidable place. It is situated in Smith Square, London, and is the headquarters of the Conservative Party Organisation. It steams with committees, research officers, regional organisers, national organisers and vice-chairmen for this and that. It is here that our hero must go for his interview. First, however, he is asked to fill out a form which makes entrance into the Secret Service seem easy. Nothing must be hidden from his past and the vice-chairman in charge of candidates will be looking for years of selfless sacrifice to the cause. The vice-chairman is a Member of Parliament, usually offered this post with a knighthood towards the end of a distinguished parliamentary career spent faithfully following the Party line. The last thing that any Conservative Prime Minister wants is a House of Commons full of questioning and unorthodox Members. Imagine the Government's programme constantly in jeopardy, the whips in despair.

Not all candidates appreciate this fact. Pringle Dempster having founded and built up five businesses over as many years, gained some degree of financial independence, married a beautiful and uncomplaining wife and spent six years on the council, decided his reputation spoke for itself. Confidently he arrived for the interview wearing a brightly coloured flower shirt and tie (in tune with the flower people's fashion of the 1960s), a blue blazer with flared grey slacks and patent leather shoes with gold buckles. Matters were not helped by the fact that the interview was unexpectedly brought forward by two hours and the interviewee had had to leave his lunch halfway through a plate of snails.

He was greeted by the vice-chairman's secretary who, realising her boss was averse to garlic, asked the candidate to wait. After two hours she came back, apologised profusely for the delay and offered him the vice-chairman's copy of *The Times*. Quarter of an hour later she returned, apologised again and asked if she might retrieve the paper as the vice-chairman had not yet read it.

Finally, the interview began. The interviewer was a man with a distinguished war record who believed it best to place his victims at a disadvantage by offering a chair the seat of which was barely six inches above the carpet, while he glared down from a great height and from behind a great desk. As Pringle sat down, one of the brass buttons from his blazer flew across the desk landing in the vice-chairman's lap, thus leaving a large expanse of flower-shirted tummy in open view. Retrieving the lost property the vice-chairman examined it and asked from what regiment it came. It was explained to him that such blazers were now widely available and could be worn without proof of military service. The button in question had originally been the property of Messrs Marks & Spencer.

The vice-chairman, by now clearly rattled, started probing into the industrial expertise of the potential candidate who told him about his great interest in worker participation and industrial democracy. This was too much for the large and now bristling figure behind the desk. Had Mr Dempster come to the right building, he was asked. Over the other side of the road was Transport House, the headquarters of the Labour Party, perhaps he had got his addresses mixed up and, if he had not, perhaps he would reconsider his views and his manner of dress before applying again.

Such humiliation is an unhappy reminder to those who enter politics hoping to break the system. Perhaps a Disraeli could get away with it, but there was only one of him. Fortunately, a new vice-chairman was soon appointed and Pringle Dempster, complete with pin-stripe suit and dark blue tie, was finally accepted on to the candidates list.

To be fair to the Tory Party this system has now been replaced by a week-end conference which resembles an interviewing obstacle course that must have been designed by Karl Popper, Magnus Magnusson and Peter Drucker. Candidates have to pay for the privilege of being interrogated and shredded before their colleagues by a group of Honourable Members specially chosen for their ability to probe any weakness, intellectual, mental and financial and who leave many applicants wondering what life must be like if they ever succeed . . .

The format for an interview varies little from constituency to constituency. The Selection Committee comprises 10 to 12 members, representing a geographical and political mix. It will include the Chairman of the Young Conservatives, a member of the Conservative Trade Unionists, and the most senior branch chairmen. The candidate will be invited to speak for 10 minutes and answer questions for a further 20. The route to success is to make the panel laugh and to show an understanding of and, if possible, a personal connection to, the local area. Pringle Dempster must imagine these 12 worthy representatives listening to their 15th speech of the day in a badly heated, smoke-filled committee room. Before them stands another youngish man in a dark blue suit regaling them on the failings of the nation, the wickednesses of the Opposition, the dangers of Communism and the idleness and incompetence of the bureaucracy. By the time they come to cast their votes their visions are blurred, their minds clogged. One man looks much like another when he is hardly visible through the haze and Oxbridge voices start to grate after six hours of repetition.

The successful candidate will keep his answers short and will try to make his speech different from the others by talking on a subject which will interest and enlighten the panel and which will not bring out the undoubted political disagreement which exists between them. The Committee must be convinced of how much he enjoys the neighbourhood and how keen he is to make his home there. If he has relatives living in the district so much the better, if he was educated in the county all well and good. At least he then has a chance of making the Committee feel that he

95

is a long lost son, seeking to return. He must do more than this, however. He should have found out the names of the most important members of the Committee so that he can address them personally. He must have discovered some of their eccentricities. 'Yes, of course, Mrs Ponsonby-Ponsonby, I am a passionate advocate of fox hunting. People must be allowed to pursue country sports without fear of Government interference. It is sad that just once in a while some of the younger, less well mannered members of the hunt forget to close the gates thereby allowing cows to roam freely on the motorway; but we all know that manners are not what they once were, although I still believe that our youngsters, given a chance, can show the world.' Such an approach will satisfy the lady posing the question, allay the fury of the farmer who owned the cows and gain the vote of the Young Conservative Chairman.

All this can be in vain, if a strong local man is putting up. There are two ways of overcoming this challenge. Firstly, he is 'local' and will not be a man of the world with wide experience of industry, commerce, local government and finance that our candidate will by now have gained. 'Madam Chairman,' he will say, 'you are looking for a man to represent South Avonside in Parliament, who may one day become a Minister, who can rub shoulders with the good and the great, not some local boy who will sink without trace in the corridors of Westminster!'

RICHARD NEEDHAM
Honourable Member, 1983

The young John Selwyn Gummer, unexpectedly promoted to be Tory Party Chairman, became, perhaps unfairly, another of those Great Comic Characters of English Literature in which the House of Commons specialises. This party conference was dominated by the problems of Cecil Parkinson, who had got his secretary pregnant after allegedly promising to marry her. But that did not prevent the chairman's mother, 'Momma Gummer', from becoming an important new figure in Conservative mythology.

Rejoice again – or at least buck up

The 1983 Conservative Party conference convened in Blackpool yesterday and loyally rallied round the politician in the controversial breach of promise case. Yes, they cheered Mrs Margaret Thatcher, even though millions of voters are claiming that she has left them in the lurch. At times like this you know who your friends are.

The only other topics which caught the conference's imagination on anything like the same scale were capital punishment and the Trade and Industry Secretary, Mr Cecil Parkinson – the mention of whose very name was enough to start a spontaneous surge of applause. In its way it is very encouraging. Hanging is an old favourite here, but trade and industry are all too often neglected.

What Mrs Thatcher, the rope and Mr Parkinson had in common was that they were not on yesterday's agenda; not even in town in Mr Parkinson's case. This gave them a great advantage over more lack-lustre colleagues and topics which were.

A succession of ministerial bigwigs, including the Home Secretary, Mr Leon Brittan, and the new boy chairman of the party, Mr John Selwyn Gummer, tried to sweep the conference off its feet. But the conference remained earthbound. This year it is unexpectedly overshadowed by falling popularity, infiltration by the Militarist Tendency and the terrifying burden of now having nearly 400 MPs, all of them with private lives and secretaries.

One could tell by the way they started the proceedings with such a dispirited rendering of the South Georgia Hymn – 'Rejoice, again I say Rejoice' – that it will take an injection of Heseltine straight into the veins to buck them up later this morning.

Meanwhile we had Mr Peter Rees of the Treasury making his first – and possibly last – cabinet speech about taxation. After Mr Rees – and possibly after his cabinet seat – came Mr Ian Gow, confidently winding up a housing debate which included the quintessential Tory line: 'Speaking as a person who started married life in a tent . . .'

And so it went on, indignant, reasonable, complacent. Representatives here who dare to oppose motions generally do so because 'it does not go far enough.' Occasionally it goes too far, but Tory conferences do not take what Mr Brittan later called 'detailed words' too literally – unlike Labour. The whingeing here is also more polite, though no less penetrating.

True, in the general tedium the conference did give a standing ovation to Mr Gummer for his competent but unremarkable first chairman's speech. But this was out of kindness of heart. Whatever doubts the activists have about the Youth Training Scheme, it is party policy and up to now Mr Gummer has only had odd dead end jobs writing speeches for Prime Ministers. He has never had a job with real security. This one may only last six months but it is work experience and could lead to a real job.

On yesterday's evidence Mr Gummer would make a good vicar.

Strangely enough it was Canon Gummer himself who kept drawing our attention to his most striking disparity. Mr Gummer is 43, but he looks and sounds about 17 and what comes out suggests that he has been 52 since he was eight.

He began a shade defensively by recalling that he joined Gravesend YCs 26 years ago, a precociously middle-aged thing to do. Next he claimed to have remembered at the time Mr Attlee's ill-fated ground-nut scheme, when he must have been about nine, the little creep. Finally, he reminisced about his Mum's reaction to the Tory election victory of 1951. 'Well, I feel much freer today,' Mrs Gummer had told her infant son. Exactly. And look where it led to: the permissive society, or trade and industry as it is known here this week.

MICHAEL WHITE
The Guardian, 1983

Julian Critchley wrote a wonderful series of four articles about the 1983 party conferences for *The Listener*. My favourite was the one which covered the Tories, who met in Blackpool that year. This was an even greater achievement, since, owing to an injury, Critchley was unable to attend, and made the whole thing up.

A few details need to be explained: Matthew Parris was a notorious 'wet' Tory MP, Harvey Proctor was the opposite. Ian Gow was then the Prime Minister's parliamentary private secretary. Sir Ronald Millar is a playwright of unblemished obscurity, who wrote some of Mrs Thatcher's speeches. Buster Mottram was a tennis player of extreme right-wing views; Kenny Everett a disc jockey who supported Mrs Thatcher.

The climax of the fictional narrative occurs on the Friday morning, the traditional end of a Tory conference. Critchley's readers were well aware that this was the day that it was learned that Cecil Parkinson had resigned from the Cabinet, having been denounced in *The Times* by Sara Keays, his mistress and the mother of his child. Critchley uses the occasion again to abuse his old enemy, Sir Alfred Sherman, another Trotskyist turned right-winger who used to advise Mrs Thatcher. Sherman's closeness to the Prime Minister and his small frame made 'The Great Mahout' a perfect sobriquet.

I returned from the Sack of Harrogate – all those burnt-out Triumph Sodomites, the smashed Doulton and ruptured cocktail cabinets – to a heavy post-bag. There was a communication from Lady Olga Maitland's solicitors suggesting an agreement whereby if I undertook not to mention their client in any of the papers in which I write, she would not include me in her column in the *Sunday Express*, and a postcard from Queretaro in Mexico with the message 'Wish you were here', signed 'Alfred'. Now, who could that be?

But there was one envelope which contained only a small square of paper, the size of a lump of sugar, on which had been drawn in pencil a black spot. This was sinister. Naturally, I wondered who was responsible. The literary allusion would exclude the bulk of Conservative MPs, most of whom believe that Robert Louis Stevenson was responsible for inventing the steam-engine.

Could it have been Chairman Gummer? I rang his secretary at Conservative Central Office, a charming girl called Fiona, who sounded handsome. She said that it was unlikely to have been the Chairman as he would have included a leaflet from the Church Missionary Society. Had I thought of trying Mr Nigel Lawson?

I did not relish the prospect of telephoning the Cabinet, from the Prime Minister's Office downwards, remembering Mr Harold Macmillan's dictum, delivered at a recently held meeting of the Conservative Philosophy Group under the chairmanship of Lord Everett of Wembley, that the Government consisted of 'a brilliant tyrant, surrounded by mediocrities'. Instead, I began to worry about the Labour Party, and how best to get to Brighton, in order to report for *Listener* readers the outcome of the big fight between Neil Kinnock of Bedwellty and Roy Hattersley of Birmingham, Sparkbrook.

Taking a leaf out of Chesterton, I travelled to Brighton by way of Newcastle, in order to appear on *Friday Live*, a late-night programme, which is the flagship of Tyne-Tees Television. It consisted of a line of pundits who had been asked to discuss the nature of opposition (Mr Michael Fallon, the Tory MP for Darlington, had been invited by mistake. it was believed by the producer that he was as 'wet' as I am), and a rabble of protesters, reflecting every grievance known to man, who spent the last half of the programme crying 'diabolical liberty'. Why is it that the Left cannot employ the word 'liberty' without this tiresome prefix? . . .

It was a dog's breakfast. Mr Joe Ashton savaged the Labour Party's policies, Mr Ken Livingstone put in a word in defence of his livelihood, while Mr Bob Clay, the newly elected Labour MP for Sunderland, lustred in pink, was not prepared to blame the party for its defeats, but rather the people, who were, it seemed, incapable of recognising a good thing when they saw one. It was a taste of what was to come at Brighton.

Miss Gillian Reynolds, who is known as the 'Iron Lady of Tyne and Wear', was in the chair. 'Did you,' she said, coming to me, 'refer to Mrs Thatcher in *The Listener* as "the Great She Elephant"?' Wishing to ingratiate myself with both ladies, I explained that in Swaziland the term is one of respect, even of admiration, being reserved for the local equivalent of the Queen Mother. But to no avail; my compliment was all over the Sunday papers, and, once again, I am in hot water. My gently satirical style should not be permitted to fall into the hands of brutal and insensitive hacks.

I arrived at Brighton, travelling on a dream ticket, late the

The Great She-Elephant.
A term of respect, even of admiration.

next morning in need of rest and recuperation. I went to English's for lunch, six oysters and a bottle of beer, and spent the afternoon looking at the antique shops in the Lanes, which were disappointing . . .

The next morning I strolled along the promenade as far as the Metropole, to attend a fringe meeting. Far out to sea loomed the grey outline of a great warship; could it be the USS *New Jersey?* The members of Labour Solidarity had gathered in the Clarendon Room, to listen to home truths from Mr Peter Shore and Mr Roy Hattersley, truths that were warmly received by what might be called the better end of the Labour Party. After a light lunch I blew 50 pence, the entrance fee charged to attend a meeting of the Campaign for Labour Democracy, held in the splendour of the Corn Exchange.

We were harangued by Mr Eric Clarke of the Scottish NUM, whose accent was so thick that, mercifully, much of what he had to say was lost; and by a Mr Deal of the Fire Brigade. Frankly, I was horrified; each assertion – for example that they were speaking in the name of the working class (surely Mrs T. has pinched most of them?) – being greeted with sustained applause. I must say, I shall look at Norman Tebbit in a new light. Indeed, I was so shocked I felt obliged to return to my modest hotel and put my feet up.

At 5.30, ignoring some old-fashioned looks, I took my place high up in the gods, to witness what the press had once billed as 'the fight of the century'. Could Neil Kinnock, the engaging Welsh lightweight with a silver tongue, sponsored by Gillette, the makers of the Dry Look, give weight away to his challenger, Roy Hattersley, sponsored by *The Listener, The Guardian* and *Punch,* known to those of his enemies who have read his recently published autobiography as the 'Immaculate Misconception'? At ringside, large men in purple pinstriped suits engaged in conversation blonde ladies who were dead ringers for Miss Barbara Windsor, while the plebs, in the cheaper seats, placed their bets, drank pale ale from cans and munched popcorn. Fraternal greetings were brought by Mr Mickey Duff.

As is now well known, the Welsh Wizard won by a mile, taking every round by a wide margin, picking up the verdicts of all three judges and the referee, four venerable gentlemen wearing dark glasses and carrying white sticks. Shrill cries of 'We wuz robbed' from those of the delegates who wore ties obliged the stewards to compensate Roy with the Deputy Leadership belt, on the presentation of which both fighters fell upon each others' shoulders in an unconvincing display of brotherly love. In Saturday's *Daily Telegraph* there was the sad story of a Mrs Maureen Gledhill, who thought she had bought a bargain when she acquired an abstract painting for £70; it was only later that she discovered that it had been painted by a duck. Could the same thing have happened to the Labour Party?

> When Critchley included the piece on the Tories in his own book, he prefaced it like this: *I arrived at Blackpool station, lugging my suitcase and typewriter. As I left the platform an aircraft flew overhead trailing a banner which read 'Maggie rules . . . OK?' I looked heavenwards and promptly tore a muscle in my hip. I was taken by taxi to my £9 a day digs, where I lay prostrate for three days, listening to the proceedings on the radio. I never set foot at the conference. Nor did I make mention of Cecil Parkinson over whose* affaire de coeur *the world made such a fuss. I 'killed off' Sir Alfred Sherman instead.*

I was seen off from Euston Station, en route for the Conservative conference at Blackpool, by none other than the editor of *The Listener*, Mr Russell Twisk himself. Did I glimpse a manly tear in his eye as the good fellow bade me farewell? He pressed comforts upon me: a packet of cheese sandwiches left over from the meeting of the General Advisory Committee of the BBC, and an illustrated book about elephants by Sir David Attenborough. It was civil of him.

Having been mugged by a gentleman from the *Sunday Telegraph*, I had taken the precaution of visiting a West End firm of theatrical costumiers. Should I travel north on the conference special disguised as a Polish cavalry officer, *circa* 1939, or as a bishop? I chose the latter, as my ecclesiastical clobber would serve to protect me from every predator, save Chairman Gummer.

The journey was uneventful enough. Rival bands of Young Conservatives ranged the length of the train searching either for

Mr Matthew Parris or Mr Harvey Proctor; Rotarians recited their rules over lunch, and the ticket-collector was pressed into selling raffle tickets. The noise from the buffet car was particularly tiresome: breaking glass, the sound of triumphal laughter and the frequent rendering of unfamiliar, martial-sounding songs. It was just like the good old days, when, uncorrupted by my peers, I would travel to Blackpool in the company of Mr Ernest Marples.

I delayed leaving the train at Blackpool when something caught my eye. I thought for a moment it was porters larking with the mails, but a small ceremony seemed to be taking place. A group of the prominenti, what Miss Jean Brodie would have described as the *crème de la crème* of our great party, had assembled on the platform as a welcoming committee.

Chairman Gummer seemed to be in charge. A silver-haired, distinguished-looking military figure, somewhat shrunken in appearance and dressed in what must have been the Latin-American equivalent of a demob suit, climbed unsteadily down from the buffet. He was embraced by Mr Ian Gow (I caught the name 'Leopoldo'), and introduced to the waiting committee. Lord Thomas, Sir Ronald Millar, whose quips have enlivened many a prime ministerial address, Mr 'Buster' Mottram, whose Conservative Political Centre lecture on the future of race relations (*Love-All?* CPU Publications) was eagerly anticipated, and Mr Teddy Taylor were, in turn, introduced to the General, who had come, as forecast in *The Listener*, to receive in person the first annual Galtieri Award for services to the Conservative Party. The moving ceremony was concluded by the singing, at the bidding of Chairman Gummer, of the first verse of 'Jesus Wants Me for a Sunbeam'.

I made my way to my very modest hotel (£9 a day), and changed into something more comfortable. Over a gammon steak and pineapple I scrutinised the list of delights contained in the conference programme of events. There was an *embarras du choix*. I might have danced the night away at the Winter Gardens to the music of the Poisonous Acolytes at the Young Conservative Ball, enveloped in clouds of blue tulle, but I thought better of all that mutton dressed as lamb. I could have paid a visit to the North Pier and seen a performance of *Fiddler on the Roof,* but I had had enough of Nigel Lawson. Finally, there was the Bow Group cocktail party at the Imperial Hotel, but the prospect of all those 16-year-old merchant bankers in Gummer glasses, talking about the money supply and urging on me the need for a resolute approach, failed to attract.

Although I have never really understood the Conservative Party, I have been hugely entertained by it. It is a tribe in which loyalty is given to the Leader (hence my 'Great She Elephant'), whose most active members assemble yearly at a seaside resort out of season to let off steam. A minority wishes to confer; that is, to push the leadership in directions which it might find uncongenial, e.g. the expulsion of black Britons; the majority, however, travel in order to enjoy themselves, to celebrate past triumphs, offer generalised support and rub shoulders with the great. It is not so much a conference, more a festival, the climax of which is the Leader's speech on the Friday afternoon.

I rose late and read the northern editions of the papers, but I set out for the Winter Gardens in good time, travelling by a circuitous route and stopping for a light lunch at Piggies (Blackpool 20803) in Deansgate Street, where I ate a sustaining pork pie just like my mother used to make and drank a glass of milk stout. The café was packed with hungry Tories eating for two, because three days at a party conference can be debilitating.

All gas and gaiters, I hurried to take my seat at the back of the hall, tucked discreetly behind a pillar. I might have been mistaken for the Bishop of Bath and Wells. I was immediately aware of what might be called 'an atmosphere'. Clearly something momentous had happened, the nature of which I was not aware. Party agents were ashen-faced, whispering together in the aisles, hearty girls who could take Michael Heseltine in their stride were being comforted by older women, and George Gardiner had given way to tears. I inquired of my neighbour the cause of this undoubted consternation. 'Haven't you heard,' she said sternly, 'Sir Alfred Sherman has passed on.'

Readers of *The Listener* can imagine how I felt. And it had happened at the hands of savages! Apparently he had been shot in the course of some doctrinal dispute in the remote Mexican town of Q——, and had been buried in the Emperor Maximilian's grave. Naturally, the arrangements for the Prime Minister's rally had hurriedly to be altered ...

On the arrival of Mrs Thatcher, the conference stood for a minute's silence. I noticed the General, supported on either side by a Vice-Chairman of the party organisation, clutching his award, which was a copy of *Margaret Thatcher, Wife, Mother and Politician* by Penny Junor. It was in this way that we mourned the passing of the Great Mahout.

What more can I say? If, in the 19th century, religion was described as 'morality tinged with emotion', a Thatcher speech is quite the reverse.

JULIAN CRITCHLEY
Westminster Blues, 1985
(First published in *The Listener*, 1983)

This was probably the best-remembered column in any newspaper from the 1987 election.

Jollying the Junta

Journalists from around the globe crowded into a small airless room in central London yesterday for a rare glimpse of Field Marshal Thatcher, legendary British strongwoman, who has held this turbulent island nation in her iron grip for as long as most people can remember.

It was the occasion of her quinquennial plebiscite appeal, an event which traditionally occurs every four years. It is one of the most bizarre rituals known to anthropologists, even against the strong competition offered yesterday by the Labour Party.

Every time it is the same. Correspondents from the advanced industrial countries as well as the local media are each handed a colourful account of the Field Marshal's heroic achievements in the glorious days since the Revolution, accompanied by threats to do more of the same. As soon as permitted, they ask about the prospects for a return to civilian rule. And every time the Field Marshal replies that she needs another five years to eradicate

106

Bolshevism and other social evils (this time it appears to be state education).

Everyone laughs a lot, but beneath the surface they all know they are witnessing a demonstration of the extraordinary power the Field Marshal has amassed. The foreign media, even holders of yen and other hard currencies, have been ritually humiliated by intense personal searches before being allowed in. They are then forced to wait for hours in conditions resembling a Calcutta January sale, inside the confines of the Blue Hole of Smith Square.

That is bad enough, but as soon as the Field Marshal appears a solid wall of enormous brutes carrying Japanese cameras rises up and she disappears from view for a further five minutes.

But the real cruelty lies in the knowledge of what awaits surviving members of her junta who participate in this ordeal. Legend has it that they used to be brought in in chains. Now that the Field Marshal's grip is so secure the style is relaxed, even jovial, but junta members know that during the process one of their number is chosen for execution.

Last time, it was a now forgotten figure called Pym, who had publicly called for small majorities. He was taken out and shot before the votes were counted, let alone cast. This time it was rumoured that Mr John Biffen had been tipped the Blue Spot for a similar coded attack about 'violence to leadership'. But he was nowhere to be seen yesterday, and inquiries elicited only vague replies that he was 'busy', on a fact-finding tour of privatisation in East Germany or 'gone to the lavatory'.

It could only mean that this Biffen had already become another of the disappeared ones. There would have to be another victim.

There followed an hour in which the pitiful wretches attempted to deflect the Field Marshal's wrath while she toyed with them in a brisk and genial fashion. 'Norman, you should be saying all this,' she would remark. Mr Norman Fowler duly blurted out a few words to the effect that he was sorry and would try harder.

'George, would you like to put it very much better?' she invited the hapless Mr Younger after making a trenchant statement on the importance of the British bomb. Only Lord Whitelaw, who has been on Death Row for many years, seemed impervious to the tension.

Some tried to avoid tension altogether. It did not go un-observed. 'I am sure the Foreign Secretary, who is very quiet, will reply to that,' the PM said at one point, a few minutes after Mr Douglas Hurd had expressed an eagerness to reintroduce the Criminal Justice Bill, 'if the Prime Minister so wishes,' and promptly taken a large gulp of water.

The Foreign Secretary, who is very quiet, said a few words and, feeling that perhaps he had not said enough, later made a grovelling plea for continuity so that the Prime Minister could continue her great work for world peace.

His position is serious. It is known that he has been threatened with a torture called 'The Woolsack', which, according to Amnesty International, produces a slow and lingering death.

The trouble with leaderism is that it is contagious. According to the opinion polls, the voters have got used to it. Consequently, those civilian parties permitted to participate in the plebiscite try to get in on the act. Dr David Owen has shown advanced symptoms of leaderism for many years, and yesterday Mr Neil Kinnock came out in something of a rash during the presentation of Labour's manifesto.

Arriving to a fanfare from 'Barry Manilow Remembers Brahms', he walked down the aisle side-by-side with Mr Roy Hattersley. Both men wore red roses in keeping with the party's commitment to florism, the creation of one million new jobs in the flower industry.

Mr Hattersley looked a shade self-conscious, as well he might. It may have been an ad-man's idea of terrific television, but in the flesh it looked like a gay wedding. Not that such notions still appear in Labour manifestos.

On the rostrum at the far end of the Queen Elizabeth II Confer-ence Centre sat members of the Shadow Cabinet, and assorted reformed hooligans brought in for the occasion. As gay wedding parties go, they looked rather too uptight to be the bride and groom's families. Rather, they appeared to be trying to pass them-selves off as the senior executives of a particularly respectable Yorkshire building society.

MICHAEL WHITE
The Guardian, 1987

Roy Jenkins finally lost Hillhead in 1987, exhausting a thick seam of comedy first worked by Frank Johnson (see page 78).

Tough life for an old gentleman

His grubby old coat battered by the fierce Glasgow wind, the old gent stands hatless in the pouring rain. To the shoppers who emerge from the Presto supermarket in Byers Road, he can offer nothing more than an outstretched hand and a ready smile.

Within the dry, well-lit interior of Presto, a Harp Lager Beer Bonanza is in full swing. Lyons mini pies are reduced to 39p and Presto Whole Orange Drink is just 49p. But these bargains are not for the old gent. The rain is his only roof, the kindness of strangers his only joy as he goes about his purpose. 'Vair nice to meet you,' he shouts after shoppers as they scuttle away from him, bags laden, backs to the wall of their hearthsides.

'I hope I may have your support,' he begs as they dash, 'I hope I may have your support.' He could tell them of better days, if only they'd listen. He could tell them of days of wine and without roses, of days when he was Chancellor of the Exchequer, president of the European Economic Community, leader of the Social Democratic Party – the lot. But they have no time to spare as they rush through the rain.

'Hello, I'm Roy Jenkins,' he said to an old lady standing by the Presto bus stop. 'Are you waiting for a bus?' Soliciting conversation from lonely old women! That it should come to this! It is as if Ralph McTell had never lived, as if the tearing and compassionate society were nothing but a forgotten dream. 'Vair nice to have met you,' he shouts after her as she hastens on to her bus.

The howling of the wind and the flashing of the rain may bite at his old brown coat, but nothing can batter his pride. His own silk handkerchief peeps out of his outer pocket. His black shoes, now flecked by the years, were once the very best that money could buy. He keeps his mind alert by approaching strangers and asking them where they live. If he can keep them talking, he surmises, they might not throw him out.

The Glaswegians of Hillhead are a friendly people. They tell the gent their addresses. 'I know it, I know it,' he replies, and then gives them full details of how to get there. They already know, of course, but there's no point in upsetting him.

Occasionally, he'll get the odd one who wants to take the discussion further, who won't stop at giving the gent his address and occupation, who frankly wants trouble. A man tells him that unemployment has always been with us. He tries to argue back, but the man won't stop. 'You won't keep quiet for a moment,' says the gent. The man continues. 'Well, that's not the view I would take,' says the gent. But still the man rants. 'Vair nice to meet you anyway,' says the gent, moving on.

Like many people in his situation, the gent really just wants someone who'll lend a friendly ear. He's not so good at listening himself, and why should he be? While an old woman goes on about the wee problem of the ugly awnings of the hairdresser's shop next door, his right hand strokes the bottom half of his face, as if signalling contemplation. As an Asian complains of roads that need repairing, the gent jiggles his left hand up and down, restless for a solution or, at the very least, an escape.

The bright lights of the Presto supermarket cruelly illuminate the puddles on the pavement. Gentleman Jenkins has been on this patch for five long years, and now they're threatening to move him on. It's not right. 'I hate the dividedness in this country,' a stranger told him. 'You've put your finger on the core,' he replies. He has to be grateful even for cores, these days.

Sometimes, you can see his mind wandering away from the problem at hand, away from the awnings and the bus stops and the road repairs to the days of long ago. Glaswegians, however cheery, are apt to come too close and poke him with their fingers while expounding on a paradox, and he is not used to such unguarded physicality. Like a member of the royal family, he releases himself by taking one step backwards, smiling, shaking their hands and saying: 'Vair nice to meet you,' his eyes already looking for a new friend.

Later in the day, he finds shelter in the Whiteinch Community

Centre on Dumbarton Road. There he parts with a dirty old ten pence piece for a ticket for the bottle stall. He examines a bottle of Bulgarian red. Might it some day be his? Alas, his number does not come up. He retreats on to the streets of Glasgow, still managing a smile.

CRAIG BROWN
The Times, 1987

Ed Pearce has done some of his best work outside the House of Commons. A critic once said he detected in *King Kong*, 'an underlying note of pathos.' Well, yes. Isn't that the point? The same underlying note of pathos is what makes this piece attractive.

The Hammersmith Soviet

There are any number of ways of spending Sunday afternoon more agreeably than attending the conference of the British Communist party in Hammersmith.

For a start Hammersmith itself is a lamentable place. As for the conference itself, well, there are things about a 65-minute speech by Gordon MacLennan, the party's decent but adagio-paced leader, which make one yearn for the crisp percussiveness of a suffragen bishop guiding the Church of England through its sodomitical dilemma.

Not that the conference was uninteresting. They were working on their liberal image, the party's recent decision to do things *al Italiano* with pluralism and free speech and other little bourgeois numbers. So of course, first of all, we had a mass expulsion.

Interestingly, despite the expulsions, a hunched little cohort of people in long-term mourning for J. V. Stalin remains. When the time came to debate final severance with the *Morning Star*, flagship (or perhaps long boat) of those former comrades in whose eyes Albania is a nest of social collaborators, we had a speech from Bert Ramelson.

For years the party's industrial specialist, notably proud in the 1970s of what he could get the TUC to do, Ramelson affects a leather jacket which suits him. He has a thick, impenetrable accent (Canadian covering Ukrainian, so I am told) and he has all the social acceptability of a man beating up his grandmother.

Mrs Thatcher should get a video made of Bert. It would confirm all her prejudices. When people talk about 'Reds under the bed' they have Ramelson in mind. With a sort of *furor ideologicus* he launched into poor Martin Jacques.

Now for people who don't follow these things, Jacques, a mild, endearing man with the manners of an archive mouse, is the best representative the Communist party has, its link with the non-party world and the producer of a journal, *Marxism Today*, which is read with attention and respect by anyone interested in political ideas.

Ramelson, who actually uses words like 'class collaboration', is a parodistic bully whose conversation is uninterrupted intimidation. In the middle of all this stand the old party regulars, like MacLennan, like George Bolton, whose chairmanship – 'Sit down, comrade, I'm not taking you' – suffers neither fools nor anybody else.

The Communist party runs now on a spectrum from Ramelson to Jacques. There is a majority of 7:2 in favour of the reconstructed approach but that majority in turn splits into enthusiasts for liberalisation and those who acquiesce. The Old Adam is there in word and gesture when it matters.

'Right, nobody leaves the room,' shouts Bolton. 'The delegation from the CPSU is here.' Up jumps everybody, including the press, which – apart from me and a chap from the Press Association – is the party press and joins in that odd clapping beloved of men in felt hats on Lenin's tomb. Comrade Viktor, translated by Comrade Evgeny (identically plump, thick-haired and metal-spectacled), conveys generalities of a complacency which would take the breath away from the Conservatives. Everybody jumps up and applauds again.

Try translating that into Tory terms (and God knows they do have affinities – I was once asked by a neighbour in Buckinghamshire: 'You do belong to the party, don't you?'). Even so I don't easily visualise Dame Pamela or Sir Basil saying: 'Now, when you are all sitting comfortably, I want your *complete* atten-

The Delegation from CPSU

tion for Congressman Pfaffenbichler who's come all the way from St Louis to explain what we must believe in this year.'

What may perhaps amaze us is that all of this is happening at all. As MacLennan scrupulously tells us, the party now has a membership of 10,350 and one town councillor, John Peck. And in spite of the best efforts of Jacques and allies like Dave Cook to make the British CP a Marx-instructed democratic party, the old, reflexive self-subordination to another country remains.

Links with the *Morning Star* group are formally ended, the Enniskillen murders were roundly denounced as 'barbaric' by MacLennan, there are people here whose devotion and unselfishness is impressive. But the bottom line is still: 'Nobody leaves the room. The delegation from the CPSU is here' – which is a pity.

ED PEARCE
The Sunday Times, 1987

In November 1987, Norman St John Stevas was elevated to the purple.

Witnessing the birth of a peer

Magnificent and swaggering in deep red and the pelts of several small animals, Norman St John Stevas was smiling to himself. He had only a few minutes more for the tawdry world of the workaday in which a chap was restricted to four names and could dress like this only for his publisher's Christmas party. He would leave this place as The Lord St John of Fawsley. Hence the smile. Soon he would be officially grander than Her. The Blessed Margaret might behave like a baroness but he was now to be officially her peer.

Flanked by his supporters, Lord Home of the Hirsel and Lord Charteris of Armisfield, he swept into the chamber. Never was a created peer so obviously born to the role. Through a long and deprived life as a commoner, in which Black Rod was only the uncle no one talked about, he had been waiting for this moment.

114

Those shirts of bilious episcopal purple had merely been a dress rehearsal.

'Her Majesty Elizabeth the Second, by the grace of God sovereign of the United Kingdom and other territories . . .' Fiji might have gone but it was still an impressive list. '. . . does admit, create prefer our right trusty and counsellor . . .' The Leaderene had never called him that. '. . . Norman Anthony Francis St John Stevas . . .' The full salute of saints' names shook like a thundersheet. '. . . Baron St John of Fawsley . . .' How euphoniously it fell upon the ear. '. . . in Preston Capes in the county of Northamptonshire . . .' Well, a little close to Milton Keynes but it would do. He was nearly a peer. He rose and doffed his black cocked hat once and sat. Twice and sat. Thrice and sat. He shook the Lord Chancellor's hand. 'Hear! Hear! Hear!' yelled all those members with the full hand of necessary faculties. Lord St John of Fawsley was born. It was sweet to see a man receiving something he so clearly treasured.

He took his seat on the government benches . . . This curious Disneyworld of democracy, a fantasy palace in which television cameras are permitted to record the proceedings and Lord Young of Graffham is called to account at the dispatch box (if yesterday's limp, prissy form is typical, he would almost certainly be mauled in the lower house). In this enchanting alternative world, Lord Whitelaw and Lord Young take turns to pretend to be Prime Minister.

As Lord St John of Fawsley must have noted with delight, the peers have the better digs – stained glass, old master wallpaper, red and gold carpet. There is a sort of ear-trumpet service for backbenchers, waistcoats are even closer to the seat in front than on the Tory shire benches in the Commons and a chap can with impunity snooze through the deeper stretches of debate.

It was unfortunate for the Blessed Norman that, having been sealed in delicious Bagehotian aspic for some six centuries now, the House of Lords chose yesterday to debate the possibility of change. Because it has no Speaker, the upper house has no formal way of telling a member to shut up. This must have been at least one of its attractions to Lord Fawsley. But, as they head towards the 21st century and the possibility of being joined by Lord

Tebbit of Chingford and Lord Skinner of Bolsover, many have felt their lordships to be in need of new procedures.

Peers have not, on yesterday's evidence, got much to worry about. Their proceedings are quite beautifully civilised. The only real problem for a new peer is to make his maiden speech even less controversial than the non-maiden ones.

Mark Lawson
The Independent, 1987

The House finally voted to allow TV coverage in 1988. I thought that this piece, more a satire on TV than politicians, captured the important point. It is not, as MPs imagine, a privilege for TV to be allowed into Parliament, but a privilege for Parliament to be awarded precious time on TV.

Wanted: men of vision

I deeply regret the decision to televise the proceedings of the House of Commons. This can only damage the dignity of television. There is no getting away from the fact that politics is basically about show business and television is bound to be tainted by this.

Just look back at the great heroes of Viewer Democracy, men and women who fought for our right to switch channels. How would they feel about the idea of permitting MPs to intrude on air time? Did people like Gilbert Harding, Muffin the Mule and Katie the Oxo Lady struggle to maintain our television traditions just for this?

There is no doubt that cameramen, having agreed to go into the House of Commons, will not be able to resist the temptation of 'playing up' to the backbenchers. You may argue that in time they will learn to ignore the presence of the MPs, but I doubt it. They will zoom their lenses and pan their cameras wildly across the scene just to draw attention to themselves. Soundmen will not be able to resist the temptation to intervene and express their views on the Poll Tax.

116

Television can be a boring and routine affair even when it is doing important and valuable work. It is not all the exciting business of directors shouting 'Cut!' and 'Roll credits!' and 'Where the hell has Ariadne got to with the coffee?' Politicians are likely to get a false idea of the working of television and will demand that the director's PA bursts into tears far more often.

The trouble is that the language and procedure of the House of Commons are quite out of tune with the hallowed, esoteric traditions of television. Call me an old fuddy-duddy if you like but I treasure those strange ways of television which outsiders often find difficult to understand.

I like the fine distinction between a 'host' and a 'presenter' (a host smiles more) and the idea that someone who watches television is called a 'viewer', but when allowed into the studio is called a 'contestant'. I know we do not use the words 'viewer' and 'contestant' in everyday speech, but it is part of the archaic charm of television.

There are other things we cannot explain, like the signature tune of the *Nine O'Clock News*, or why that cat always appears sunbathing on the shed roof during the opening titles of *Coronation Street*, or why weather forecasters are traditionally comic characters, or what newsreaders say to each other when they straighten out their papers at the end of the bulletin. These are mysteries, but it would be a black day if they were ever streamlined or rationalised.

Strict guidelines will have to be laid down. I have been kicking around this problem for some time, having lengthy conferences with senior people in broadcasting, going out for brain-storming sessions in bistros and setting up numerous sub-committees.

The important thing is to find a format. Every television enterprise requires a format. I see the coverage of the House of Commons procedure as being a subtle combination of a chat show and a quiz programme.

For example, the front benches on the Government and Opposition sides will be renamed Celebrity Panels. Each Minister and his opposite number will sit at raised plywood desks and each one will have a buzzer to press when he wishes to speak. The buzzer will, of course, also light up his name and constituency on the front of the desk. ('Well interrupted, Birmingham Sparkbrook.')

The rest of the furnishing of the Chamber (or studio, as it is properly known) will have to be changed. Those green leather benches are hardly appropriate to the dignity of the television occasion. Tubular aluminium swivel chairs convey much more of the flavour of statesmanship. There will also be sofas for when Ministers appear as 'guests' at Question Time.

'Good evening, my first guest this evening is the Minister for Cracks in Paving Stones.' (Hugely enthusiastic applause.) 'Well Minister, I must say you are looking very dapper tonight. I gather you are about to publish a Paving Stones (Standardisation) Bill. This is very exciting news.'

'Thank you for the plug! Yes, everyone in the Ministry is tremendously excited about this one. I am looking forward to the Third Reading.'

'If I may slip in a quick supplementary here, Minister, that is a jolly attractive shirt you are wearing. Is there, perhaps, an amusing anecdote concerning this shirt?'

'How clever of you to guess. Yes, it was given to me by my very, very dear friend, the Minister for Light Bulbs, during the committee stage of the Socket (Adequate Provision) Bill which, as you know, had a very long and successful run.' (Studio audience goes wild.)

For more emotional occasions, such as the Budget speech, there will be stools. These are the tall precarious stools which American singers perch on at the end of the show when the lights go down and they wish to be confiding and a little sentimental.

Of course, it goes without saying that most of the major Ministerial speeches will be mimed with the sound dubbed over because of the acoustic difficulties at Westminster.

We must also ensure that the actual presence of the cameras is obvious. The fashion in television is for the viewer to be able to see all the hardware in the studio to give him the impression that he is somehow being allowed behind the scenes, so the cameramen, lighting and cables will be in vision all the time. This is a response to the public's demand for more Open Television and insistence on understanding all the workings of our Viewer Democracy.

118

In place of the Speaker, we shall need some figure with real authority, gravitas and a sense of history about him. In other words, a Floor Manager. He will prowl about the Chamber wearing headphones, carrying a clipboard and making severe winding-up gestures if anybody is guilty of un-televisual conduct or of impugning the honour of the studio audience.

Perhaps if we stick to these rules it may be possible to see that the great institution of television is not manipulated by the presence of Members of Parliament. It would be a black day indeed if Parliament became the master and not the servant of television. It would be more calamitous than the shooting of J.R., the departure of Hilda Ogden or Valerie Singleton leaving Blue Peter.

OLIVER PRITCHETT
The Sunday Telegraph, 1988

Great events in the Commons, such as the 1988 Abortion bill debate, rarely live up to their billing. It takes a lot of resource to turn these essentially non-existent affairs into tough, readable, worthwhile copy.

Passion and fury give way to ticking of the clock

As the minutes ran out, Sir Bernard Braine, Father of the House, stood in his place on the Tory backbenches, staring at the Chamber's green digital clock, head bowed, eyes hooded, hands clasped as if in supplication, in a final prayer vigil for David Alton's Abortion Bill.

The clock, the silent but most deadly of their opponents, was within ten minutes of defeating them.

Sir Bernard – old enough to recall the television panel game *Beat the Clock* – will remember it as a formidable opponent. Five hours earlier he had been eyeing it with the respectful suspicion of an old trooper as the countdown started.

295 minutes to go: proceedings begin. The dignified part of the constitution, Mr Speaker Weatherill, is challenged by the undignified part, Mr Heckler Skinner, with a point of order. Dignity prevails.

119

287 minutes: The first of 12 petitions opposing the bill, procedural spanners in the Alton works, are presented and read out. Among the petitioners is one of the deputy hecklers, Brian Sedgemore.

Mr Sedgemore does his best to get his Cockney around the antique parchment language – many honourables, showeths and humblys – but the general effect is Sid Yobbo reading Shakespeare. His petition read, and having served its purpose, it goes into an elegant dustbin, a green sack at the back of the Speaker's chair.

215 minutes: This morning of 'passion and fury' – as Mr Sedgemore has described it – properly gets under way. Morality and conscience – mortgaged to the party whips on any other day – are returned to their owners for the morning.

Some MPs – Clare Short against the Bill and Ann Widdecombe for it – show effective passion. Only David Steel and Tony Newton, for the Government, used persuasion.

Mr Alton spoke in adjectival ketchup, spraying his opponents with 'barbarism' and 'corruption'. Minds – where the protagonists would admit that their opponents ever had them – were not so much made up as encased in lead, poured over with concrete and buried six feet under.

134 minutes: the first – and least consequential – amendment at last goes to the vote after a marathon speech against the bill from Ann Clwyd.

The public gallery is packed, among those present Glenys Kinnock, Lord Longford, several women in Stop Alton's Bill T-shirts, clergymen and nuns. At one point there is a deep-throated cry of 'bastard' at one of Mr Alton's opponents. You trust it isn't one of the nuns.

54 minutes: David Alton makes his second speech, sacrificing most of it in an attempt to save his bill. He is again the impassioned, pious, holy figure, appealing for a better world, in the role popularised by successive Popes. Mr Alton is less successful in the part. Nor have his tactics, particularly the stubbornness over offering compromises to his opponents, been as infallible as his supporters hoped.

42 minutes: Clare Short begins a passionate attack on the bill, by turns angry and sad, but most of all very long.

120

32 minutes: David Alton interrupts Clare Short to plead for a motion to close the debate and move to the vote. After two failed attempts by his supporters to drive the bill into the division lobbies, only a miracle can save it.

God in this context is a Yorkshireman – Deputy Speaker Harold Walker. He is not disposed to grant one.

'There are still opinions to be heard,' he says.

20 minutes: Cyril Smith finally wrings closure out of Mr Walker. 10 minutes: Sir Bernard clasps his hands in prayer.

0 minutes: Time has run out. The private line to the Almighty is either out of order or otherwise engaged.

ANDREW RAWNSLEY
The Guardian, 1988

Craig Brown here describes what makes the sketch-writer's job easier – the fact that politicians' jokes are generally so unfunny. When they are amusing, they tend to depend on more background knowledge than most people care to possess. See Bernard Levin on page 14.

Jokes that are no laughing matter

There are quite a few jokes cracked in the Chamber of the House of Commons, and quite a bit of laughter, but the two are rarely connected. Jokes are followed by silence and serious statements of intent by laughter. In theatrical terms, it is as if Hamlet's every soliloquy were to be greeted with gales of merriment, whilst the comical antics of Mr Frankie Howerd were to cause rivers of tears.

In this higgledy-piggledy arena of muddled humanity, a Labour speech detailing horrendous atrocities in Chile will provoke much mirth on the Conservative benches. The Labour benches match this mirth, chortle for chortle, at the sight of Mr John Moore stuttering his way to early retirement. On the other hand, when such an obviously absurd character as Mr Roy Hat-

121

tersley rolls his tongue around one of his immensely humorous Yorkshire adages, the House looks utterly funereal.

Sir Geoffrey Howe did not reach the position of Foreign Secretary by cracking jokes. Far from it. He wouldn't last more than a couple of seconds at the Glasgow Empire, unless, of course, he pretended to be someone impersonating Sir Geoffrey Howe. Yet in the House of Commons, he has them rolling in the aisles. After Ms Clare Short had accused him of duplicity over the Palestine Question, he replied: 'We do not have double standards in that respect', and even Members on his own benches began clutching their bellies and guffawing fit to bust. 'Nor in any other respect,' he added, but it was too late: HO! HO! HO! HO! HO!: Gentleman Geoffrey couldn't be heard for the laughter.

A while later, Mr Jeremy Corbyn, who looks rather like a hippy undertaker after a hard day's work, rose, grim and unsmiling, to list imprisonments and disappearances in Turkey, his voice solemn and monotonous. The club of rowdy young Tories just couldn't stop laughing, whispering fresh jokes to one another, their red, well-oiled faces flickering in the afternoon light.

These underpublicised young Tory rowdies might be well advised to seek help from a Television Charm School before the coming of the cameras, for their particular brand of raucousness is unlikely to gain them the adulation of the general viewer.

Mr David Mellor had been sitting on the front bench waiting to answer a question for a full half-hour, so he obviously felt that his eventual appearance should be heralded by a small joke. 'They also serve who only stand and wait,' he tittered. Alas, a small joke from Mr Mellor has the effect of a full Requiem Mass from anyone else . . .

But this complex and intriguing survey of humour on the benches would be incomplete without a reference to two Members who are funny both in intent and in effect. The first is Mr Dennis Skinner, whose rasping, cackling jokes, though perhaps better suited to a smoky Soho basement than to the venerable Chamber, always manage to raise a smile from all but his immediate victims. More and more, he relies upon Mr Speaker as his fall-guy ('just a moment, just a moment, don't get excited' is the well-loved Skinner catch-phrase) before turning his razor tongue towards the day's most complacent Minister. It is generally supposed that Mr Skinner will have to clean up his act before the cameras are admitted, but this is a nonsense: he stands to become a major TV folk-hero, a sort of comical Robin Hood.

The other natural comedian is Mr Tony Banks, whose merry quips can lighten the most tedious of afternoons. Sadly, when Mr Banks puts his jokes behind him, the effect is ruinous, for his serious opinions tend to be shrouded in killjoy glumness. Thus, he cracked a good joke at the beginning of his speech: 'May I remind the House of the miracle of the Wedding Feast, when Christ turned water into wine. Now, he could have turned it into Nestlé's cocoa, but he chose to turn it into wine.' But, as he rambled on, it became clear that he was proposing a bill to attach Government Health Warnings to alcohol. Dear, oh, dear. It was a sad day for British Comedy.

CRAIG BROWN
The Times, 1988

After nine years, Mrs Thatcher has become an expert Parliamentary stonewaller, the Geoffrey Boycott of the Commons.

No question of a straight answer

THE READER: *Would the column find time in its busy day to consider the matter of whether or not the Right Hon lady the Prime Minister is capable of answering a straight question?*

THE COLUMN: In the vast majority of all cases – yes, the vast majority, and I can only assume the reader is making so much noise because he doesn't want to know the answer . . . In the vast majority of all recorded cases, this column is able to give a full, yes a full, answer to questions of this kind. In the report of the Columnar Interrogation Reply Rate committee, chaired by Professor Eric Sinecure in 1984, the committee concluded . . . Yes, I *will* sit here and type it all out, word for word, if that is what the readers opposite want . . . the committee said: 'There is no substantive evidence to suggest that the rate of interrogation reply, per capita, allowing for the necessary weighting, has in any way diminished in recent years.'

THE READER: *The column seems not to have completely understood the question. Let me ask again. Is the Rt Hon lady the Prime Minister capable of answering a straight question? Yes or No?*

THE COLUMN: In the second appendix to the Sinecure Report, the committee concluded: 'The evidence of recent years, with regard to the reply rate of questions of the nature specified within the remit of this inquiry is that neither nor more less inquiries . . .' Oh, yes, I am, I certainly am, going to type it all out again . . . 'neither nor more less inquiries can be proved to have been answered satisfactorily within the period under investigation than can be shown to have been the case in any other comparative period'. As far as I am concerned, considerably more questions have been answered in the lifetime of this column than in a lot of other columns I can think of.

THE READER: *Is she capable of answering a straight question? Yes or No?*

THE COLUMN: I am certainly not going to take lectures from the readers opposite on the subject of answering questions. Before 1979, in the Winter of Non-assent, it was perfectly normal to find unanswered queries, hints not picked up, abandoned questions lying around in the columns of Great Britain. We have increased the possibility of a questioner getting an answer, we have increased the range of available responses, we have maximised the rate of interrogation response to a level never dreamed of before and certainly not by the readers opposite. The rate of reply to direct questions is *up* to 75 per cent; to indirect questions *up* to 84 per cent; *one hundred per cent* of rhetorical questions are now answered, compared with only *forty-two per cent* in pre-1979 columns.

THE READER: *Yesterday in Prime Minister's Question Time, Mr Hattersley, deputising for Mr Kinnock, asked Mrs Thatcher three*

124

times whether her government would fund in full the nurses pay settlement. Did she reply?

THE COLUMN: This column has written on very many previous occasions about the funding of the nurses pay settlement. On the 18 February 1988, page six, column two, we wrote – oh yes, I am just going to sit here and copy it all out again – 'Mrs Thatcher again refused to answer any direct questions on the funding of the nurses pay settlement.' I have absolutely nothing to add to my previous statements.

THE READER: Mr Hattersley asked Mrs Thatcher twice to answer his question 'Yes or No?' Did she answer him? Yes or No?

THE COLUMN: The rate of reply to direct questions *up* to 75 per cent. To indirect questions *up* to 84 per cent. If the readers opposite want statistics, they can have statistics. It's no good writing 'yes or no?' like that. I've written many times before and I am quite happy to write again . . .

MARK LAWSON
The Independent, 1988

INDEX OF CONTRIBUTORS